T0132280

OPEN YOUR *Greatest* GIFT

Granted On Delivery

DEBRA DOMINO

BALBOA.PRESS
A DIVISION OF HAY HOUSE

Copyright © 2020 Debra Domino.

All rights reserved. No part of this book may be used or reproduced by any means, graphic, electronic, or mechanical, including photocopying, recording, taping or by any information storage retrieval system without the written permission of the author except in the case of brief quotations embodied in critical articles and reviews.

Balboa Press books may be ordered through booksellers or by contacting:

Balboa Press
A Division of Hay House
1663 Liberty Drive
Bloomington, IN 47403
www.balboapress.com
1 (877) 407-4847

Because of the dynamic nature of the Internet, any web addresses or links contained in this book may have changed since publication and may no longer be valid. The views expressed in this work are solely those of the author and do not necessarily reflect the views of the publisher, and the publisher hereby disclaims any responsibility for them.

The author of this book does not dispense medical advice or prescribe the use of any technique as a form of treatment for physical, emotional, or medical problems without the advice of a physician, either directly or indirectly. The intent of the author is only to offer information of a general nature to help you in your quest for emotional and spiritual well-being. In the event you use any of the information in this book for yourself, which is your constitutional right, the author and the publisher assume no responsibility for your actions.

Any people depicted in stock imagery provided by Getty Images are models, and such images are being used for illustrative purposes only. Certain stock imagery © Getty Images.

Print information available on the last page.

ISBN: 978-1-9822-4466-8 (sc)
ISBN: 978-1-9822-4468-2 (hc)
ISBN: 978-1-9822-4467-5 (e)

Library of Congress Control Number: 2020904709

Balboa Press rev. date: 03/09/2020

To all the people and characters who inspired this manuscript. Thank you very much for your support and encouragement to write another book. You are truly inspirations. This is to all the dimensions that may have connected to form the power for this purpose. This is a positive intention and affirmation that all of your visions become manifestations for self, others around you, and the world to see. Whether magically, miraculously, intellectually, or viscerally, may your visions unfold saliently as your greatest gift is revealed and delivered. Let it shine.

Contents

Introduction

What is a gift? A gift is an offering that is given or bestowed voluntarily. Gifting is the act of giving a present. The word present means a time that is now and the exact moment. The word present also means to be alert to circumstances, attentive, ready, and available. Another meaning of the word present, pronounced pre-zent, is to introduce with a formal announcement or ceremony. Presenting can be done in the form of a performance, a story, or a drama.

Think about how it feels to receive a gift that you love. It can be something that you enjoy doing. It can be something that you need to help fulfill a particular goal or desire. It can be something tangible that can be touched and seen and that feels real. A gift can also be intangible. Intangible means it is incapable of being apprehended by the mind or senses. It can be something unable to be defined. Something intangible can be an asset that gives power even though it cannot be touched physically. It is there spiritually or emotionally to give inspiration, power, and energy.

What if there is a bounty of gifts stored somewhere, like a treasure chest just waiting to be opened by you?

Where is this hidden treasure? Once discovered, what if you were presented with the opening of your greatest gift? When and where is the gift delivered?

Open Your Greatest Gift takes a look at ways to tap into the scripts encoded at birth with the initial voice of the sound. The cry that welcomes the baby to the world can be the key to seeing the brightest light to shine the way through the journey of life. It just takes practice and daily commitment to learn how to do it. *Open Your Greatest Gift* explores how to meet the day-to-day challenges by using a soundly constructed platform. There are steps, stories, and examples to guide the way to open the gifts.

Let's explore this concept with your imagination and a deep analysis of your self-contained characteristics and see what unfolds.

PART I

The Delivery

The anticipation and the wait for this most auspicious moment has been surreal. The pain at first was so scary, like something never felt before. It was shocking, the labor in preparation for the parturition of a new creation of life. The act of love, the conception, the months of gestation, the biological changes and nurturing, the emotional trauma, and now it is time to deliver. Then the crescendo of the initial voice to the world arrives. The auditory cry radiates all around to deliver the sound. The cry is the sound of the baby's first voice to the world. The birth process is the formal presentation of the new life to the world.

The bundle of joy arrives pure, innocent, and filled with many keys and treasures, without the sins that await in the shadows. The parents usually wait to cuddle the miraculous new bundle, a precious collaboration of the mother and the father. The mother and father have already been on the journey, navigating the trails of discovery. The family now has a new member added to the team of explorers. This becomes a huge responsibility yet also a huge opportunity for the family to grow together as the nurturing process begins. Each family member has a role that contributes to the harmony of the family. Each parent has been through the delivery process with their own birth into the world. Each parent has a head start on the new child that has arrived. This makes their role as the leaders of the family so very important and pronounced. Years before, the parents echoed their cries to the world with their own entry and delivery. It is the cycle of life that continues to repeat itself over and over, again and again. It is the great infinite gift of life with the potential to keep on giving the gift forever.

The Gift of Parenting

The entry into the world, the birth, is the presentation of the gift. The announcements are made about the birth of the new gift that has been delivered. The initial characteristics of the height, weight, length, and the time of birth are recorded for the official announcement and the birth certificate. The present moment is captured with the history of the birth of the new baby. It can be a time of great joy and celebration. It can be a time of anxiousness with thoughts of what happens next. It can be a time of general reflections about life and the new journey.

Any parents reading this, stop and think about the feelings you had with the birth of your first child, your second child, your third child, or after each birth. Did you realize what a great gift had been delivered to you in that moment? Did you think about having a support system in place for guiding your child through the discoveries and challenges of life?

At my college graduation, my mother hugged me with tears in her eyes. She was shaking her head in disbelief that the day had come for me to graduate from college. She shared with me what her thoughts were after my birth. She said that she held me in her arms and whispered a sincere prayer to ask God to please let her live to see her little girl graduate from college. She went on to tell me that she saw no way at that time that she would be able to send me to college because she had no financial resources. She had only faith and hope that a way would be made when the time came. I received a full all-expense scholarship for college upon my high school graduation, and that was how the way was made. My mother said that the sound of the scream that came from me when I entered the world was so loud. She said she could not wait to see what she had delivered with that loud cry. That moment in time was a gift for me. The look in my mother's eyes and the proud emotion that she exhibited made me feel like I had really accomplished something great and that my mother had believed in me from the first time she heard my cry to the world. That moment made me feel like I had opened the gift of the next chapter of my life. I felt so much love. I felt determined and motivated to continue making my mother proud. It became the story of my life to go out and accomplish things that my mother was not able to accomplish during her lifetime.

My mother entered the world in the year 1919. During her lifetime, formal education systems were limited. The educational teachings that my mother had were probably the equivalent of an eighth-grade education. That is why she prayed and wished to live to see her baby girl receive a college education. The emotion from my mother made me feel blessed to live during a time where education systems were available to provide the opportunity to achieve and to build better lives for my own children and the future generations. The gift of education can be a tangible and intangible present. That graduation day delivered a type of awakening for me. It was the realization that there is formal education, and there is parenting education. They go hand in hand to complete the total package for the support system to navigate the terrain of life. My mother may not have had a lot of formal education, but she had built her own educational system made of the values of strength, character, love, morals, beliefs, dedication, faith, hope, and perseverance. These intangible values are gifts, and the collection of the presents made a support system that my mother instilled in me.

The Family Support System

One of the keys to building a quality life for children is having a strong support system where the children can learn and grow. Each family structure may be different. For example, after the birth and delivery of the new baby, the child comes home to meet the rest of the family. The family unit is like the core group, the hub for growing and nurturing the new life to maturity. It may consist of the mother and father and other siblings. Sometimes it is a single-parent home and consists of just the mother. There may be a grandmother, grandfather, aunts, uncles, cousins, stepmother, stepfather, godmothers, godfathers, and so on. Whatever the structure consists of and the number of people living in the home, the opportunity is there to establish a strong support system. The support system is key to the child's quality of life and necessary for taking care of the child's basic needs. The financial health of the household is key to the strength of the support system. The support system also consists of day-to-day teaching and training the child mentally, physically, and emotionally. All these supports are keys to the child's growth process in each phase of life. Establishing the components of the support system and working together in the family every day to perform the duties can also cause growth for the parents. Maternal and paternal instincts kick in, and they are ready to perform as the need arises. A new life and the need to care for the life can cause strengths to appear that may have been unknown. It becomes the natural response to handling the new responsibility.

Let's begin with a very basic need that shows up right after the delivery into the world. The baby feels the yearning for food and immediately knows what to do, just by instinct. The question of what to do does not need to be pondered. The baby begins to wail, using natural intelligence to cry for the mother to bring food. The mother responds right away. Handling the process in this way every time the need arises activates the powerful feelings of love and security for the baby and for the mother. The bond grows stronger each day. These are very strong values for the family support system.

The maternal instinct comes naturally, as it was conceived in the mother's birth from her mother, and it grows stronger as the mother births her own child. The process of feeding continues from childhood and into adulthood as the mother naturally continues to pull resources together to provide food and nourishment for the family. Other family members may participate in the process. Sometimes the father is the provider of the food, and sometimes other siblings or caretakers may provide the food.

At each growth phase of the child, the support system may need to grow. It depends on the situation and the needs of the family. It is the process of day-to-day life. The success and overall development of each person depends on the values instilled by the family support system. The education process begins with the teachings from the mother and father.

When the child is born, it is unknown just what their future life will consist of. The support system is the grooming process. The home family support system lays the foundation. As the child develops, observations from family members are important keys to determining the strengths and characteristics. Sometimes raw talent may be observed at an early age. The way the child learns and responds to instructions can help determine the mental aptitude and attitude. The observations are important so that decisions can be made to help prepare the child for the next phases of life and adulthood. The observations may help with decisions about what type of school the child will attend. Monitoring and taking care of the mental and physical health is very important. The growing years from childhood to adulthood go by so fast. That time is a gift to cherish and enjoy each day. The growing years can be so much fun for the child and the parents. The child can feel secure because the parents provide for them and take care of their needs. The parents may feel complete because the child has brought so much joy and happiness to their lives.

The day finally comes when the child has grown to a stage of independence. This is the time when the child realizes that they have grown to be an adult and have to make their own choices or decisions. The challenges and shadows of life show up in the form of day-to-day problems and obstacles. This can be a difficult time in life, trying to find the best way to handle and conquer each situation.

The next section offers a solution—tapping into the inherent resources that have been developing inside since birth. The challenges of life come with the opportunity to use the natural resources stored inside. The resources may have been inherent from birth and might be strengths inherited from your ancestors. There may be strengths developed from the family support system or learned intelligence from various educational systems. The strengths of each person are the characteristics, traits, or scripts than can be used solve problems and make sound decisions. Tapping into this internal think tank or reservoir is like using a personal sounding board or building a platform to handle any situation by using and defining your own gifts.

The Sound Platform

What if there is a bounty of gifts stored somewhere, like a treasure chest just waiting to be opened by you? That was the question asked at the beginning in the introduction. Let's try to find the answer to the question.

Tap into your think tank and try to remember your birth day. This is the day that you were delivered into the world. Do you remember any thoughts that you had once you exited your mother's womb? Well, if you can remember any details from birth, then you are an extreme genius. Even if you do not remember, it does not mean you had no intelligence. The sound of your voice in the form of the first cry was your natural, inherent intelligence and response when first delivered. You had a voice then, and you have a voice now. The initial sound of your voice had meaning. However, it was not defined as a characteristic at the time of birth. The strong characteristics were hidden within your DNA, waiting to rise during the growth stages in your life. These characteristics and inner strengths make up your personal sound platform.

Each new life brings new meanings and discoveries waiting to be harvested. The emphasis on the sound of the baby's first cry stakes the claim. The sound of the voice states the intention to have a sound mind and heart, upon which to build a strong foundation.

The platform for the journey of life was delivered turnkey and portable, with many keys inside. The sound keys are the descriptors that define the script to access when needed during the journey of discovery.

The portable system is carried inside your vehicle for life, which is your human body.

The keys are the emotional intelligence stored inside. The keys are the descriptors to help along the way and to define the scripts. The scripts become your statements that identify who you are and give you authority to do and be whatever you desire. Many new scripts may be discovered along the way, as the intelligence has a way of revealing itself when the need arises. The supply comes when the demand arrives.

The sound platform is your personal sounding board for navigating day-to-day issues in life.

For example, think about a situation or challenge you are going through. There is nobody around that you feel comfortable sharing with or asking for advice. It feels like your back is against the wall, with the wall being the only source of support. You feel all alone, with nowhere to turn. You may speak, but no other physical person is in the room with you or anywhere near. You know that you must do something to face the challenge at hand. The mental thoughts, analyses, and invisible barriers around you become your personal sounding board or the platform to sustain you. Deep inside, a thought may come to mind, and that thought may lead to another thought. Then you find yourself making it through the next hour, or next day, or next week. The answers to the problem have begun to reveal something that may not be the final solution, but it leads you on the path to a resolution. It can happen without the feeling that progress is being made.

The components of the foundation provide the anchors for sustaining and building the quality of life. They are the defenses against attacks upon the structure of the vehicle of life and all that is contained inside. The dark shadows of life show up to bring the negatives, the opposite effects, and to impede upon the strengths planted soundly within the foundation. Some of the traits are buried inside people, even if they do not realize it. Sometimes situations in life can cause different emotions and descriptors to turn on and many more to reveal themselves.

On the journey of deciding what to do during some of life's seemingly complex situations, let's explore the process using the what if, how to, and sounding board resources from the platform, the solid foundation gifted to life. The sound construction being described here may be referred to as the "sounding board," "sound platform," or the "foundation." Metaphorically and with connections to inner spirituality, it is meant to describe the progression of birth from the silence in the womb to the vocal entry into the world, to the tangible movements and actions of navigating and exploring life using the initial sound of the voice. The initial sound of the voice makes a sound contribution in the sense of being solid, concrete, and steadfast for the journey of life. That is the intent of the human experience. The sound or voice progresses through to adult life. It has a huge collective purpose of multiplying and advancing the world so that the physical life experience can be like heaven on earth.

Each time the platform is used and the resources provide the necessary support, growth takes place. New discoveries, scripts, and meanings appear. Thoughtful expressions occur to form new axioms, sayings that inspire to keep going and do more. The key descriptions that define the meaning and purpose for life and the characteristics of each character are referred to as the scripts. In essence, these scripts are like a treasure chest filled with gifts, waiting for you to discover them so as to help you get through situations. These scripts can help you to open your greatest gifts, which will guide you to live and build the best life for yourself and others.

Debra Domino

****Please add your own identifying scripts if your
descriptors are not found in the table below*****

The Sound	Platform	Scripts
Bold	Able	Adventurous
Caring	Analytical	Assertive
Confident	Authentic	Beautiful
Conscious	Aware	Blessed
Content	Compassionate	Compatible
Dependable	Complete	Conscientious
Evolving	Courageous	Creative
Experienced	Deep	Empathetic
Faithful	Determined	Energetic
Fit	Effectual	Entrepreneurial
Friendly	Enthusiastic	Fair
Futuristic	Focused	Flexible
Gifted	Forgiving	Fluent
Good	Fruitful	Generous
Happy	Heartwarming	Giving
Healthy	Honest	Grateful
Humble	Hopeful	Hearty
Kind	Intelligent	Important
Light	Intuitive	Influential
Loveable	Legal	Ingenious
Optimistic	Levelheaded	Instinctive
Organized	Outspoken	Loveable
Peaceful	Persevering	Loving
Productive	Positive	Observant
Ready	Powerful	Outgoing
Respectful	Profound	Passionate
Safe	Purposeful	Patient
Secure	Quiet	Pure
Skillful	Reasonable	Qualified
Smart	Sensible	Resourceful
Solid	Social	Sincere
Spontaneous	Soulful	Talented
Stable	Spiritual	Talkative
Strong	Steadfast	Unstoppable
Trustworthy	Thankful	Visionary
Unbroken	Undamaged	Well grounded

Steps to Using the Sound Platform

Each person's story is unique. Each situation is unique. In that perspective, it is up to each person to figure out the *how to* by analyzing the why, how, and what the desired want is. With the sound platform model, here are some steps that can be taken to help with the process:

1. Get to a quiet place and space so that you can communicate with yourself.
2. Try to relax and take some deep breaths, getting as comfortable as possible.
3. Honestly ask the questions of *why, what,* and *how.* It may be a time when you are in a situation and are asking why? What am I going to do? How will I get through this?
4. Listen to see if you can hear an answer.
5. Breathe deeply and see if you get a sense of a special feeling or emotion.
6. Go inside yourself to your very own sound foundation and define the scripts that describe it.
7. You may refer to the scripts shown on the sound platform in this book. You can choose as many as necessary to describe what you feel truly represents you. Add other scripts if your definition is not found on the sounding board in this book. The scripts are what describe your overall characteristics and abilities.
8. Think of the obstacle at hand.
9. For each script that is chosen, state and stake your claim, beginning with the words "I am." State your name and then your

scripts. For example, "I am (your name). I am bold, determined, focused, ready, sincere, and loving.

10. Now think of and state clearly the intention of what you want and desire to accomplish.

11. Now, go back to step 9 with your "I am" statement. Add your intention statement to the "I am." For example, "I am (your name and then your scripts). I am bold, determined, focused, ready, sincere, and loving. I desire to turn my life around by focusing on my purpose for life. I want to fall in love with my life and write my own romantic love story, which will build the business that I have dreamed of."

12. Each day, commit to an action that supports your scripts and your intentions. Remember, your actions should not cause hurt or harm to yourself or others. Make it fun, as your essence begins to glow.

13. Keep repeating day after day and make a journal of your progress. You may even make a set of goals or action statements and update your list as progress is made. Just remember to keep committing to this each day to keep moving forward.

Keep in mind that was only an example. Fill in the blanks with your own desires. Remember, be true to *yourself*—not what someone else desires or intends to do.

The following is a simplified version of the process, in just three steps:

Three Step Process to Using the Sound Platform

1. Define and claim your purpose or intention.
2. Define and describe your scripts, your abilities, your strengths, your statements of your character, and your defined values to be used and put into motion to reach the desired intention or goal.
3. Take the first step into action.

The next steps sometimes unfold to give you direction for how to do the next action. Just keep repeating the steps as new directions or revelations show up.

As you get used to staking your claims to who you are and what you can do, it becomes invigorating, and a sense of power takes charge. New meanings sometimes show up, giving clarity and new direction. Also, the more this is practiced, the more it becomes intuitive and is done unconsciously. It is done without realizing that it is being done. It becomes a natural part of your being, and turning it on is like shining your light. The switch just turns on automatically.

Introduction to Story Section

The next section contains stories that have been inspired by real-life events. The details in the stories show how different characters face real-life challenges. The characters make decisions about how to handle the problems that present themselves. The stories are a way of showing how people naturally use their internal scripts and instincts to meet and conquer the different challenges that show up in life.

Before we go into the next section, I want to share a way that I used the sound platform as an activity with a group of young kids.

I was very nervous because I had accepted a position to substitute for a teacher in a subject area that I had never done before. The subject was engineering and technology. Believe it or not, I sat in the car, rocking from side to side as I connected to my own internal scripts. "I am analytical, experienced, qualified, and sincere. My intention is to do the very best I can with the students today and learn as they learn. I will get through this day successfully—so, nerves, settle down!"

When I got to the room to review the notes and objectives that were left by the teacher, I smiled. She had made it so clear, and I had an idea. The instructions were to build a project for the community that was environmentally friendly and would help the people of the community using the Legos building blocks. The many different Legos were on a pushcart that was used to go from room to room for each class. When I got to the first class, I learned that the students were very familiar with the process and knew what to do; however, I was concerned that if I did not find a way to engage them and put myself into the process, I might not have order in the classroom. That was when the thought came to me to use the sound platform for groups. The schedule of classes went from kindergarten through fifth grade.

I instructed the class to break into groups of five. Depending on the size of the class, some groups had four students, and some had six. I instructed them to come up with a name for their team. I gave them instructions to introduce themselves to me and tell me what they would do to help the team build the best project for the community. Each student followed instructions, and they went to work building the projects. I could hear them talking among the groups and giving instructions like little leaders of the future. It warmed my heart so much to watch them in action. I felt like I was the student.

After the project was finished, each group had to choose their spokesperson to present the project for the team. I told them to speak clearly and state their name and team name. Those students really got into the project, and the sounding board seemed like a new way to teach and make it fun. Those students proudly stated their scripts. There was so much energy and determination in each classroom, and each of them felt that their project was the best. I could not believe how creative those young students were and what they presented to me. Nearly every group used the scripts of being *strong* and *smart*. One group wanted to use two spokespersons. They said it was because one was the strongest and the other was the best speaker. I will tell you that they made a true believer out of me. Even the students who appeared quiet and shy participated and stated what they had to bring to the project. The sounding board worked perfectly and was so much fun. The descriptors made great spelling words and also great words to be used for writing essays. Some of the projects that they came up with were brilliant. If presented as ideas to councils in the community, no one would have known that they came from elementary students.

At the end of the day, I went back to my car but not before going to the sounding board to say, "I am *thankful.*"

What if there is a bounty of gifts stored somewhere, like a treasure chest just waiting to be opened by you?

I felt that a bounty of gifts had been opened, with many fruits from the seeds of the community, those smart and strong students. I also felt inspired, stronger, and more confident. I had a feeling that I needed to use the building blocks inside of me to construct a new platform for my own life visions.

The next section is about life stories that unfolded and were inspired by real-life events. See how the characters used their internal sounding board characteristics to help them get through situations.

PART II

The Inspiration of Stories

Many situations make it seem like there is no exact way to conquer day-to-day life; there is no model for how to handle many situations that come up. Situations just show up, and strength and patience are required to navigate them and get to the solution. Sometimes action is required on the spot. Things can unfold right before your eyes—unexpectedly.

This section is based on inspiration from real-life stories. The stories are from my personal, direct, and indirect life experiences. Artistic interpretations have been used to dramatize and characterize the essence of each underlying challenge. While the stories are inspired by events in the storybook of my life, fictitious names have been used, and fictitious characters and situations may have been added to further dramatize the story line.

Stories are life's way of being an open and continuous book, and often, each person has input in the way their chapter is written. That is the purpose of tapping into the strengths and definitions from each unique sounding board of characteristics and strengths.

The Cry for Help

The auditorium that seated five hundred people was filling up fast to listen to the famous sounds of the Celebration of Life Orchestra and Concerto. The music event usually pulled large crowds each year.

A young woman walked into the auditorium lovingly carrying a baby. She took a seat and started to feed the baby. After a few minutes, the woman moved to the next row of seats behind the initial seat she had chosen. The procession started with the band playing the most beautiful and melodious tune. The event was about to start as the crowd anxiously awaited. The sound of a baby fretting with irritation reverberated from the row where the young woman was seated. The facial expression of the woman showed restlessness and worry. The ushers assigned to the duty of seating and directing the guests to their seats were actively, attentively, and proficiently fulfilling their responsibilities.

"Whoa!"

"What was that?"

The sound of a loud scream escalated to drown out the beautiful music, and the rustle of movement and distress filled the air. The frantic sound rang out loudly and clearly, along with the crying of tears and the word "Help!" The woman ran out of the auditorium to the foyer area. Footsteps pounded the floor as several of the ushers ran behind the young woman to see if help was needed. The baby seemed to be choking on some type of foreign object or liquid. The young woman had weakened and had fallen to her knees on the floor, with the baby still in her arms and in distress. Instinctively and spontaneously, the ushers gathered around the young lady. One of the ushers, a seemingly seasoned mother or grandmother, grabbed the baby and did some type of maneuver. It may have been the Heimlich maneuver. It just happened so fast. Within seconds, spittle and other mucous were barfed from the baby's mouth onto the floor. The baby started to cry, and the problem seemed to be stabilized and resolved. The young woman continued to cry but with tears of joy and relief, with words of gratitude to the women who came to the rescue.

Breakdown of Key Components from the Story

In this situation, the sound platform delivered the resources of *instinct, spontaneity, caring, helpfulness, observance, compassion,* and *determination* to handle the situation. The young woman with the baby may have been a new mother, and this experience granted a lesson learned. The shadows tried to intervene and muddle the natural instincts of the young woman, but there were helpers who had access to their own internal sounding boards, and they were prepared to perform on the spot as needed. The helpers immediately organized to form an emergency trauma team, a triage. This is also a testament to the beauty of the cycle of life. Each person involved in this story was part of the initial delivery process, with their own births containing the treasures inside. Now many years later, the fruits of the labor performed to save another life. This also shows the power of a loving and caring spirit. That act shows how the gifts were opened. The light was the skills of the helpers, granted on delivery and opened to save the baby. Instinct, spontaneity, and love save lives.

Intuition Baby

The beautiful red and golden leaves rustling on the ground, whispering welcome to the autumn season, felt so warming. It was a bright, sunny day in 1969 in a small rural town in the South. The hot summer had made its exit, and the fall season was in session, along with the new school year. Big plans were in store for the school that year. Rebecca, the lead third-grade teacher, was ready to roll out many new ideas. The end of the summer had been so much fun as Rebecca reflected about the summer vacation and camping trip.

Rebecca breathed in some fresh air as she got into the car, anxious to pick up her precious little three-year-old son from her mother's house. It was a long day at school; she felt drained and could not wait to get home. As she drove into the yard, she saw Johnathan peeking out of the window and waving to her. His puffy cheeks and autumn-colored hair blended in with the curtains that draped the window seat. The happy look on his face was like the sun shining on a dark night. It made her so happy, and she forgot all about feeling tired and drained.

Johnathan ran to get a big hug, just as he did each day when she picked him up. His eyes seemed to grow as big as teacup saucers, with a slight glisten. He said, "Mommy, you have a booboo. Did you hurt your arm today?"

Rebecca looked at her left arm and saw a blue mark that started where her hand connected to the wrist and went up about two inches farther. Rebecca said, "Well, that's just an ink mark from an ink pen.

You know that Mommy works around pens and pencils all day, so you may see marks sometimes on my clothes. Mommy is okay, so let's get home to hug Daddy and eat our family supper together; then I will tell you a fun nighttime story before bed. Johnathan started jumping up and down and clapping, as he could not wait for the fun nighttime story.

Dinner was delicious, and story time was enjoyable as always. It was also very effective, as Johnathan fell sound asleep soon afterward.

Rebecca went into the bathroom to shower and get ready for bed. She noticed that the ink did not wash off her arm while bathing. It was also startling to observe that the ink mark had traveled almost to the bend of her elbow. Rebecca thought that was very strange. She also noticed that she was feeling even more drained, and it was slightly different from the normal workday drain. She thought she should probably go to the local emergency room to get it checked out. She told her husband, Dan, what was going on and asked him to stay home because she did not want to wake up Johnathan. She also did not want Johnathan to worry, since he was the one who had noticed the mark.

By the time Rebecca had checked into the emergency room and was assigned to a room, the mark had moved a little bit farther up her arm. The hospital team immediately started taking blood to run tests.

Finally, the doctor came in to report to Rebecca that he wanted to admit her into the hospital overnight. The diagnosis was that she had a bacterial infection. The doctor said that he wanted to prescribe antibiotic steroids intravenously to get it stabilized. He also informed Rebecca that she had come in just in time. He told Rebecca that if the infection had continued to move farther up her arm and closer to her heart, it may have poisoned her bloodstream. Rebecca burst into tears as she thought about Jonathan and how he was the one who first saw the ink mark as harmful. It was like that little boy was the first responder, and the intelligence was packed inside a simple, little, chubby-faced boy. Rebecca was thinking, "How could this happen?" Yet it happened, and she would be fine. Rebecca went home the next day. The doctor mentioned that she may have been bitten by some type of poisonous spider. It appeared that her immune system was attempting to combat the infection. It had not been moving too aggressively. Rebecca thought about the camping trip and thought that may have been where she encountered the spider.

Rebecca could not wait to get home to see the cutest and smartest little genius in the world and to get many hugs and kisses. She felt so proud to be a mom.

Breakdown of Key Components from the Story

Now in this story, many scripts were used from the sound platform by Rebecca, Johnathan, Dan, and the team at the emergency room. Each person involved used the values to *observe, react,* and *solve* the problem even though the problem did not reveal itself as a problem initially. It was the *intuition* and *observation* from the three-year-old boy that made the discovery. Rebecca realized that there might be a problem after the ink did not wash away during bathing. Dan was the supportive father and stayed home with Jonathan while Rebecca was in the hospital. Each person was part of the team and used the scripts from the sounding board. Discoveries make possibilities and lead to even more discoveries. This discovery was a savior that prevented another problem from devastating the young family. That young family exhibited many of the qualities essential for the making of a bright future. These inherent qualities shine brightly and clearly on the sound platform. The gifts were opened successfully in this story. *Intuition and observation are visionary eyes.*

Golden Feet

Little Elgin Brannon was the second-born child in a family of four. He was not as outgoing and active as his brother who was two years older. There were two other older siblings, two girls who were adopted into the family. Elgin was quiet and mild mannered. Even though he had an older brother still young enough to play with and older teenage sisters, Elgin seemed to enjoy playing alone in a corner by himself. He seemed to have the most fun laughing to himself like he had his own comedy show going on in his head. He also enjoyed family dinnertime. He loved to beat on the table or on his high chair, as if he could hear drum beats and music in his head. He enjoyed eating his food, and most of the time, he asked for more. Everything seemed normal about Elgin. There was only one problem, yet the doctor seemed to think it would work itself out. Elgin had not learned how to walk, and his second birthday had come and gone. The doctor said that Elgin had a slight case of genu varum, the medical term for being bowlegged. It was only a slight bow though, so the doctor predicted it would cure itself during the growth process. Everything else checked out to be normal.

Elgin's mother started a new job and needed to place Elgin in a day-care facility while she worked. Egin's mother looked at many different facilities and disclosed to all of them the problem with Elgin not walking. Everything else was normal, and he could crawl around fast. He could also pull up to chairs and hold on to them and take basic steps, but something was preventing him from walking on his own. Finally, Elgin's mother went to a place that felt like the right place. It was warm, and the entire staff seemed compassionate and friendly, with strong motherly instincts. It was a rather small and cozy center inside a church. Elgin's mother registered him to attend the day care.

Elgin seemed to adjust right away. He went to a corner and started playing by himself, in his own world. Elgin's day care teacher/attendant, Valencia, was a young friendly lady who had recently graduated from college and moved to the area from another state. She did not have children, but she said she came from a large family, and she seemed to be very good at bonding and connecting with the children at the center. Each day when it was time to pick up Elgin, Valencia had a full report of the day. Things were going very well, and Elgin's mother was so happy that she had chosen that day care center for Elgin.

One month before Elgin's third birthday, Valencia met Elgin's mother at the door as she was just about to enter the facility. Elgin's mother got a little nervous, wondering if something was wrong. Valencia started jumping up and down with excitement and said she had something to show her. Elgin's mother thought maybe she had observed Elgin beating out music on the table or something. But, drumroll—what a sight to see, glittering like gold! Elgin came running to his mother without holding on to anything. Valencia was in tears, and so was Elgin's mother. They hugged and did the happy dance all around the room. Valencia then started to tell Elgin's mother how it all happened. Elgin was in the corner playing and having fun by himself. He pushed a chair away from the table as if he was trying to grab it to stand up. But oh no, oh yes, he did not need the chair! He stood up and started taking steps. He then looked down at his feet like they were made of gold and started laughing, as if thinking, *This can't be! You mean these things can move like this?* Then he started high stepping around the room while looking down, admiring those feet. He just could not stop looking at his feet, like he had discovered gold at the end of a rainbow, and it belonged to him and no one else. Elgin's mother could not wait to get home to break the news to the rest of the family.

Valencia had some more news to share. Elgin's breakthrough had caused a transformational breakthrough for Valencia as well. Valencia had been stuck in a situation. She had gone to college, but she could not find any work in her field that she enjoyed doing. The work experience at the day care center and witnessing Elgin's breakthrough had given her clarity, and she knew what she wanted to do. Valencia decided to go back to school to get certified in learning and physical disabilities for early childhood to elementary-aged children, and she wanted to start her own school. She went home and right away started charting out the plan of action. She really felt that she could contribute to society by making all disabilities full abilities.

Elgin's third birthday party was a blast. He could not only make music beats in his head, but he could dance on those golden feet. He was the star of his party, and the family could not believe the fortune and joy everyone was feeling around this breakthrough and Elgin's success.

Breakdown of Key Components from the Story

This story pulled from many of the scripts. It was like Elgin had been born with special instructions to bring about a transformational experience that involved his seeming disability, which was only temporary, with the destiny of helping Valencia see her purpose in life with full clarity. Valencia naturally used many of the scripts with her *friendliness* and *compassion* for children. She was also very *attentive, observant,* and *kind.* It was as if there was a preorganized purpose for Elgin and Valencia that was ordained by a greater spirit, a bigger power that guided the way and time. It knew the exact time to turn on the scripts. The delivery was granted, and the gifts were opened. *The journey of many miles begins with the first step, and that could be a golden step.*

The Will of the Skill

Doritha Kneelings fell to her knees and begged Ronnie to reconsider what he was planning to do. Even though Ronnie was considered a grown man at the age of nineteen years, Doritha always seemed to be protective of Ronnie. He was her firstborn son of five children. She was always concerned about his behavior. She felt that he would always need his mother by his side.

Ronnie, however, had a different opinion of himself. What his mother may have been picking up on was the feeling that he did not belong. Ronnie felt like there was something different about him and that he did not fit in with his other siblings. It may have been because he was the firstborn and was made to work the fields with his father. His father was a farmer and needed the help of his oldest son to keep the farm going. Ronnie had no proper school training, just training at home, working the fields. His education was equivalent to a fourth-grade level or less, compared to normal children getting a full high school education.

Ronnie did not back down and held strongly to what he really wanted to do. Ronnie threw both hands up in the air and exclaimed, "Mom, I am in love with my girl, Eillean! She is pregnant with my child. I just want to be a man about this and take care of my own family. I want to marry Eillean. She is my soul mate, and she loves me. Things have been so hard trying to work the farm with Dad. Dad acts like he hates me for some reason. The more I try to do, the more he gets upset. Mom, don't worry. I will be okay."

Doritha was shaking her head, and tears fell as she said, "You do not have any formal education or skills. You know nothing about running a household! Ronnie, please come to your senses. Can you even count to twenty?"

Ronnie stated, "I will find my own way! It will work out!" He turned and walked out the front door with a flour sack bag of clothing hanging over his shoulder. Doritha Kneelings fell to her knees and screamed for mercy. That day felt like the end of the world for Doritha. She felt like she had lost the thing that made her complete, being the protector of what needed to be protected. The house felt empty without Ronnie, but Doritha knew she needed to concentrate on raising and supporting the rest of her children so that they would not falter and go astray.

Twenty years went by. Ronnie's parents passed away in that time that Ronnie was away.

Ronnie found his niche to be working on cars. The hidden skill just showed up. One day, a car had stopped in front of the house where Ronnie lived. He went out to see if help was needed. Instinctively, he immediately knew exactly what to do. He got the car running and on its way within the hour. Word got around about Ronnie's skills, and people started bringing their cars to him to fix. He became the shade tree mechanic and had a home-grown business. People brought old cars to him that were barely running. If they seemed unrepairable, Ronnie kept the cars for parts as needed. He continued working on the cars and continued learning until he eventually had repaired all the cars that were not working. It turned into a used car lot after a while. Many of the people who left their cars there, assuming they were unrepairable, never came back to pick them up or to check on the status.

Ronnie was making more than enough to take care of his family. The skill and raw knowledge to fix the cars seemed so natural, as if he had gone to formal training to learn. He had learned how to build a car from scratch. He had made so many designs of parts. He envisioned that he would make a new generation of car lines. He had designed the mechanics to make a window roll up and down automatically. He also had a part to make the engine run smoother and faster. He had a bumper made of scraps, but the materials would cause a car to bounce right off another car in case of a crash. It seemed like Ronnie was creating these inventions right out of the future. Sometimes he sat and pondered all the things that he had done and wondered how he had discovered how to do them. He wondered if he had lived once before, working on cars, and had come back to life in the body of Ronnie Kneelings.

One day, a man came into town and went to the shade tree car shop to visit with Ronnie. He told Ronnie that he knew of a fellow from upstate that wanted to see some of the new inventions he had designed. He thought that Ronnie could get paid a lot of money if he sold his ideas and inventions to the fellow that was coming to town. He told Ronnie where to go and meet up with the fellow on the following Tuesday. Ronnie was so excited. He could not wait to share the news with his wife, Eillean, and for Tuesday to arrive.

Tuesday finally arrived, and Ronnie drove off to meet the fellow. It was at a service station in town. The meeting went very well, and Ronnie agreed to turn over his inventions to the fellow for a very nice compensation package. It involved taking care of his family until all the children were grown. The contract was contingent upon Ronnie continuing to create new designs and inventions to be sold to the fellow and his company exclusively. Ronnie agreed and signed the contract.

It was late in the evening when Ronnie headed for home. The sky was dark and dreary, and the moon was nowhere in sight. As Ronnie turned the curve, another car came speeding out of nowhere, like it had the fast engine Ronnie had designed. Ronnie tried to turn the steering wheel to get off the road, but the car he was driving did not have automatic steering. Boom! There was a crash.

Ronnie awakened in the hospital. He had lost a lot of blood. The doctor asked if he had another family member who could give blood. Ronnie's mother and father had passed away years back. He still had two of the four other siblings that lived in town. They went to the hospital to attempt to give blood, but none of them had the same blood type as Ronnie. Ronnie's blood type was AB positive. All of the other siblings had the blood type B positive. Ronnie had a rare type of blood that carried the antigens of both A positive and B positive.

It finally made sense to Ronnie what was going on. He must not have been the biological son of the father he thought he knew. He had to have a different father from the rest of his siblings. That was why he felt like he did not belong. That was why his mother was so protective of him. She took that secret to her grave. He wondered how it had happened. He wondered if his father knew the truth. He thought he must have known or felt something because neither he nor his father seemed to enjoy working with each other on the farm. That was why he had the strong will to leave and go on his own, even though it did not appear that he had any other skills. This was truly an awakening.

The fellow who had set up the deal to buy the designs from Ronnie came to the hospital to see if there was anything he could do. As it turned out, he had the same blood type as Ronnie. He offered to give blood, and his blood was a perfect match. As it turned out, it appeared that he might be a relative of Ronnie, possibly on the side of Ronnie's biological father.

Ronnie made a full recovery and could not wait to get back to working on cars. Eillean was pregnant with their third child, and he needed the support and compensation promised to him from the signed contract. Everything seemed to come together. It was the deep-seated will inside Ronnie that made him walk away and pursue his own life with Eillean.

The fellow stopped by within the next month with the first payment per the contract. Ronnie had already completed another design. Ronnie observed that the man seemed like he had stuffed a pickle or something in his throat, and he was sweating. Ronnie asked him if he needed some cool water or needed to lie down in bed. The man finally said, "I have something to tell you." Ronnie got nervous. He thought that the deal might have dead-ended and he might not get the compensation promised. The man took a deep breath and reached for Ronnie to hug him. He said, "I think I am your biological father. Your mother was the first woman to hold the key to my heart. We made the decision to part ways and keep our relationship a secret. Son, we will talk, and I will tell you everything." Ronnie was in shock and felt like the wind had been knocked out of him.

Breakdown of Key Components from the Story

Now this story had some surprising revelations. Somehow life manages to make a circle, and what is unknown becomes known. What happens in darkness comes to light. This story tapped into the scripts of the unknown, and the *will* and *skill* scripts were pulled—possibly from way back in the history of Ronnie's family tree. But just see how those skills came to life. It was Ronnie's *strong determination* to leave home and start on his own. It was just what was needed to sustain Ronnie, despite not having a formal education. Everything that was needed had already been blueprinted inside of Ronnie. The scripts unfolded in a very prosperous way. The gifts were granted and delivered. *Skill and will can help to provide sustainability.*

The Silent Healer

The family had been called in to say the final goodbyes to Edison Rampsey. It was April 1973. It had been more than thirty days, and Edison remained in a coma. The medical diagnosis was that Edison had some type of cerebrovascular accident that had caused swelling in the brain. It was described as a massive stroke. The doctor said that it could strike like a silent killer. The chaplain at the hospital came in to give words of comfort to the family. Darkness seemed to drop the shroud of a veil over the room to announce that the darkest hour had approached.

Melanie Parker sat and held her best friend's hand to provide comfort. Sabrina Rampsey leaned over on Melanie's shoulder and started to weep. Sabrina was Edison Rampsey's youngest daughter. It was the month of April, and Sabrina just kept thinking about the fact that she would not get to dance with her father for the father-daughter dance that would be held in June before Father's Day. Melanie was thinking about how different things would be not seeing Mr. Rampsey's face greet her when she got on the school bus each morning. Mr. Rampsey was the school bus driver in the community. Melanie and Sabrina were twelve-year-old students in seventh grade.

It does not seem fair, Melanie thought as she felt the pain of her very best friend since the first-grade tug at her heart. Melanie hugged Sabrina tightly, and Sabrina started to weep harder. The tears wet Melanie's blouse like it had been drenched in a rainstorm. Melanie closed her eyes and thought about the situation. She started to see Mr. Rampsey in her mind, smiling and saying, "Good morning, girl! Come on and get on this bus." She could feel the warmth of a type of spirit that seemed to dry the wet tears from her blouse like a warm fan blowing hot air on her. Melanie had a bright idea. She asked Sabrina to stay there with her in the room with Mr. Rampsey for the night. She wanted to just sit and talk about normal things with her best friend, as if life was normal. She also wanted to join hands with her best friend and pray every hour around Mr. Rampsey's bed.

After the other family members had left the room, Sabrina and Melanie stayed. They went down to the hospital cafeteria and got some snacks and quickly went back to the room. They sat and played simple childhood games and talked about the fun times when they were little girls. Mr. Rampsey would pick them up and run as fast as he could with them on his back, and it felt like a joyful horse ride. They looked over at the bed at Mr. Rampsey. He appeared to be quietly asleep in an unconscious state. They ate snacks and invited Mr. Rampsey to eat with them. They even put some crackers up to his mouth and pretended that he was eating with them. They joined hands and prayed each hour as planned. They played the game of patty cake. "Patty cake, patty cake, baker's man, heal my daddy as fast as you can." They broke some crackers into pieces, spread them over Mr. Rampsey's lips, and declared that it was bread falling from heaven to feed the medicine needed to heal. They planted the most sincere and loving kisses all over his forehead and cheeks. They rubbed his legs and tickled his toes. At one point, Sabrina thought she saw her father smile, but she then realized it was probably her imagination.

Sabrina had to admit that her best friend had had a good idea. Sabrina had forgotten about how sad she was earlier in the evening. It almost felt like they were at home with her daddy up and well and in the other room, listening to them play and have fun like they had done for so many years since the first grade.

The time flew by as they camped inside the room. They had fun, and it seemed like the fun lifted the dark veil that had dropped into the room earlier in the evening when the family had been called in to say the final goodbyes. Sabrina looked at the heart monitor and saw that her father still had a heartbeat going strong. That gave her hope as she felt the love and support from her very best friend. For some reason, Sabrina felt that they were not alone. She could not explain it. It was a weird feeling she had. Sabrina could not find the words to describe what she was feeling because it did not make sense to her, but she knew it was something different.

Finally, she felt herself dozing off to sleep. Melanie was sitting next to her in the other chair, falling asleep. Sabrina started dreaming. She could hear her father talking to someone and laughing in the dream. Sabrina then floated to the window as if the force of gravity took her into outer space. She saw fluffy clouds that broke into pieces like crackers and then turned into many little cells that came together to form a blanket. The blanket started singing the most melodic song, and Sabrina started to drift deeper into sleep. She heard her daddy saying that he had to get to Pete. Pete was the family's first dog. He showed up to their house when Sabrina was in third grade. He had no collar and seemed to be a stray looking for a home. Pete ran away two years later and had not been seen since. Then Sabrina heard alarms going off. She was thinking, *Oh, we're having another fire drill at school.* Sabrina then felt Melanie touching her, trying to wake her up.

Sabrina realized that the alarms were coming from inside the room. She could not believe her eyes. Her daddy was moving around in the bed, trying to get out. He had pulled the cord from several of the monitors that were attached to him. He seemed to be saying, "I've got to pee!" Several nurses ran into the room, as the monitors had signaled the nurse's station that there was a problem. Sabrina and Melanie were standing there frozen and speechless, trying to interpret what was happening. The head nurse asked the girls to leave the room so they could get Mr. Rampsey stabilized. Both girls burst into tears and ran to try to find a phone to call home to tell the rest of the family to get to the hospital as soon as possible. Someone from the hospital had already called, and Sabrina's mother informed her that they were on their way.

The family arrived at the hospital, and everyone was in the room along with the doctor. The dark veil had been lifted. Mr. Rampsey had awakened from the coma. The head nurse reported that she had gotten him up from bed earlier that morning and helped him walk to the bathroom to urinate. Sabrina thought about her dream of hearing him say that he had to get to Pete. Then she woke up to the alarms in the room and thought she heard him say that he had to pee. Her ears had not fooled her. Her daddy was actually speaking. She was hearing him speak inside of her dream and also for real right from his sick bed. Sabrina thought he was saying he had to get to Pete, but he was actually saying he had to pee. Sabrina thought, *Did Pete help Daddy come back to life?*

Everyone in the room was crying tears of joy. The doctor informed them that there were more tests to be run and that he would need to stay at least three more days in the hospital, depending on the test results. However, the doctor said that he believed a recovery was very much in sight. A miracle had happened.

Mr. Rampsey was discharged from the hospital after three days and sent home to relax and recover. Sabrina felt that there was nothing that could not be done if you just asked for it, believed it in your heart, and had a very best friend like Melanie.

Mr. Rampsey made a full recovery and was able to attend the father-daughter dance. He was also asked to be the guest speaker to give a testimonial of his experience and recovery. He titled his speech "The Silent Killer Met a Silent Healer." He told the story of Sabrina and Melanie camping inside his room at the hospital. The crowd gasped in awe as he described what happened. He could hear them in the room and had witnessed all the things they were doing as they prayed for him every hour and kissed him until they finally dozed off to sleep.

Sabrina gasped and said to herself, "You heard us, Daddy." The story was a miracle. Mr. Rampsey could hear even though he appeared to be unconscious and unmovable. Yet there was something else. Sabrina wondered if that was what that strange feeling she had felt in the hospital room was trying to tell her. The entire room was cheering, and it seemed like cheers were coming from outside too and all over the community as the word of the miracle spread across the town and to surrounding towns.

The dance seemed like something out of this world, like a fairy tale. Sabrina wondered if she was still dreaming and would awaken soon. When her daddy pulled her onto the floor for the very special father-daughter dance, he hugged her so tightly and kissed her on the forehead, just like she had done to him in the hospital. She then knew that it was for real and that she was not dreaming. She just could not stop thinking about the words, "The Silent Healer."

Breakdown of Key Components from the Story

Now this story is really one to remember. It embeds that memory of the miraculous day when something shifted in a big way. The sound and concrete platform supported the cause, and it held up strong and steadfast in a magnanimous way. Sabrina, Melanie, Mr. Rampsey, and all the other supporting characters tapped into many of the scripts from the sound platform, and it all came together. *Faith, hope, love, determination, perseverance, creative, ingenious, positive, supportive, caring, compassion*, and many other visible and hidden scripts showed up for the miracle. The gifts were opened and delivered. *Expect a miracle every day.*

Mothering by Appointment

Diedra stood in the hospital room staring at the precious bundle of joy that she had birthed just a short while ago, it seemed. She felt so blessed and happy. It had been a hard pregnancy. Diedra had been sick almost every day with morning sickness. The sickness seemed to never stop throughout the pregnancy. Initially, before she realized that she was pregnant, she thought she was coughing up mucous from a sinus infection. It had been such a stressful and painful journey, but the pain and lessons learned were worth the gift of the joy that she now felt in her heart.

It had not been easy for Diedra. The conception had taken place during a time when unwed mothers and sexually active young girls who did not save their virginity for marriage were persecuted. During the early years of the twentieth century, some people had self-righteous beliefs. Diedra's mother had declared that Diedra would go straight to hell for not keeping her legs closed. Diedra did not know what to do. She had heard of a lady in town who could possibly help get rid of the pregnancy, but she could not wrap her mind around doing it and did not know how to get it done. She had no money to pay the lady, and she had nothing to barter with for payment. She thought about going to hell and realized that the situation at hand felt like a state of hell. It was so painful to see her mother so angry with her.

Diedra sat under the large oak tree in her mother's backyard. She started thinking about things. Diedra felt that she was a good person. She was smart and had always gotten good grades in school. She had potential. She had never bullied or caused harm to anyone else. She had much love in her heart to offer her child. How could being pregnant be the worst thing in the world, when her mother had been pregnant with her? If her mother had not birthed her into this world, she would not be here now, pregnant at the age of seventeen. She asked God for forgiveness and to please help her and show her what to do. She made a promise to herself and to God that she would strive to be the very best person she could be for the rest of her life, if she could just get through this pregnancy. She promised to work hard so that she could make the best life possible for her child. She asked sincerely, from the bottom of her heart, and spoke loudly. She opened her eyes and realized that she was all alone, talking to the oak tree. It seemed that she had dipped out into another world.

Deidra wondered what her father was like. Her mother told her that he died when she was six months pregnant with her. Diedra realized that she had not seen any pictures of her father and had not questioned why. At least Diedra knew the father of her baby. It was her first love; she had fallen hard for the star football player. After the first kiss, she could see everything she ever dreamed of in the stars that floated before her eyes. She melted at his touch. Now pregnant and all alone, Diedra felt sad. The father of her child had moved away to another state up north. He had other family members living there, and they informed him that there were more opportunities to find a good job there. He had come to the house to say goodbye to her, but Diedra's mother had met him on the porch with a broom cocked over her shoulder like a shotgun. She had dared him to step up on her porch. She told him to get out of her yard and never set foot there again. That was the last time Diedra saw the father of her child. Diedra wondered if something similar had happened with her mother. Maybe that was why she was being so hard on her, because she hated to see a repeat of her own life. It was just a thought. Diedra decided to tuck the thought away to the back of her mind.

The day finally arrived a little more than seven and a half months later, just shy of eight months. Deidra screamed to her mother for help.

She thought she had a urinary tract problem because she had gone to the bathroom but could not stop the flow of urine. "I can't stop peeing, Mom! Please help. Something's wrong." It had been going on for more than five minutes, which felt like forever and was really scary for Diedra. Her heart felt like it was about to beat out of her chest.

Deidra's mother softly said, "It's time to go to the hospital. It looks like your water has broken."

Diedra panicked. By the time she made it to the hospital, Diedra said that she had to use the bathroom again. She said it felt like she had a lot of stool to push out, and it felt painful. She asked if she could have a stool softener to help. She went to the bathroom, as she thought she was having a regular movement. Yet it was another type of movement; the baby was pushing down and on the way. She was in full labor, and the baby was making its way into this world sooner than expected. Deidra had almost delivered the baby right into the toilet before the medical staff came into the room and rushed her to the delivery room.

Finally, the arrival weighed in at two pounds six ounces. A little baby boy screamed the sound to the world, "I have arrived." Landon had landed. He stayed in the hospital for six weeks in an incubator because he was born early, underweight, and his heartbeat seemed a little irregular. Diedra was so scared and worried. She could not wait to get her baby home and to begin her journey as a new mother. Landon needed treatment from the neonatal unit before he was released to go home. He was released six weeks later, weighing five pounds six ounces. The journey as a new mother had finally begun for Diedra.

Now thirty-six years later, Diedra was standing in the hospital room admiring that handsome two pounds six ounces bundle of joy that she had delivered—seemingly a short while ago in her mind. Now standing six feet three inches tall, Landon was so brave, handsome, and intelligent. So much had happened over the years, yet time seemed to fly by. The birth of her son was the best thing that could have ever happened to Diedra, despite the initial hardship and scandal when she first got pregnant.

Dr. Landon Therous Cummings was a third-year resident at the hospital. Diedra's mother had been given approximately forty-eight hours to live. Landon and Diedra were by her side. Landon had become the apple of Diedra's mother's eye soon after he had finally made it home from the hospital. Landon even referred to her as "Mama." The scare from the premature delivery seemed to shake the reality in Diedra's mother's mind. She realized that she was blessed to have a grandchild. She had taught Landon so many valuable things, and Landon adored her spiritual wisdom. Landon and Deidra said their final goodbyes. They expressed their heartfelt sentiments of how much they loved her through all the ups and downs. With tears streaming down her face, Diedra passionately said, "Mom, I would not want to change my life to happen in any other way." Deidra declared her as the best mother ever and thanked her for all the tough love she had given her. Landon held his grandmother's hand and asked her to keep watching over them. He told her that he would always honor and remember her, and he vowed to continue doing research to find a cure for that dreadful disease before the end of his life.

Diedra's mother gave a final order with a very weak voice. She told Diedra to find her older sister. She had gotten pregnant with her first child when she was seventeen, just as Diedra had done. She had given her first child away to the preacher and his wife. They had moved away to the West Coast to build a new world gospel church twenty years ago. She then said that she was ready to join Diedra's father. Even though he had gotten her pregnant and started dating her best friend, she always loved him. She weakly whispered that she would whip him with the broom, and then her eyes went still. Diedra broke down into tears as Landon held her.

Breakdown of Key Components from the Story

Oh my! It looks like Diedra has some work to do after planning the funeral and burial. This story has so many scripts and dark shadows intertwined. Diedra's early commitment to God while talking under the oak tree pulled many of the sound scripts. She declared that she was *good* and *smart* and would be the very *best* she could be. She was *able* and *willing* to make the best of the situation. She worked hard to be the best mother possible for Landon. Diedra's determination was instrumental for her family because her mother had changed and realized that the birth of Landon was just what their small family needed. Landon grew up and used many of the scripts, along with being motivated by his grandmother's scripts of wisdom and spirituality. This story is also a testament to the fact that many times scripts show up by appointment, and it is difficult to understand the trial of the appointment when it occurs. It was Diedra's destiny to conceive Landon, and Landon had the appointment to use his gifts to help the world. The scripts can chain together throughout the generations. It is as if the scripts self-organize to resolve situations that did not manifest to fulfillment in a past life. Yet the delivery was granted, and the gifts revealed themselves. *The trial could be the miracle for your destiny.*

The Secret Message Delivered

Theodore Raysford and his wife, Donessa, headed down the long hallway at the special needs center to see Theodore's brother Tarvis Raysford. Tarvis was forty-two years old. The center had called the family because Tarvis was in critical condition. There had been some type of reaction between the medicines for his behavior disorder, the pain medicine, and the blood pressure medicine. Theodore and Tarvis were the only surviving siblings in their family. Theodore was ten years older than Tarvis. Theodore kept close watch and visited the special needs home to spend time with Tarvis every day. Tarvis was devastated and lonely after the loss of his wife, Mayvette, the year before. Tarvis and Mayvette had met at the state special needs school and had gotten married twenty years ago. They seemed so compatible and lived together at the special needs home.

As Theodore and Donessa turned the corner to go into Tarvis's room, the door was closed. Theodore opened the door and did not find Tarvis in his room. He went to the central facility desk and was told that Tarvis was rushed to the medical center next door. The center was very big and exclusively for special needs patients. There was the general psychological center, the medical center, and the special needs home that housed the active mental and physical patients.

When Theodore and Donessa arrived at the medical center, they were escorted to the family counseling room and informed that the doctor would be in soon to give them the report on Tarvis. Donessa consoled Theodore, as it was apparent that the situation had shaken him up pretty badly. Theodore was thinking about his painful past. Something tragic had occurred forty years before.

Donessa looked at Theodore and knew that he was thinking about what happened forty years ago. Theodore usually had bouts of depression and sadness over it. Each year on the date that it happened, Theodore would get emotional. He just could not get the memory out of his mind because there were so many unanswered questions, which made it difficult for Theodore to find a resolution and closure. Theodore was the oldest brother. There were four other siblings—three brothers, including Tarvis, and one sister. Theodore thought about the day it happened. He had gone to stay with his grandmother for the weekend. His mother kept the remaining siblings at home with her. Two of his brothers were age eight and six. Tarvis was two years old, and the baby sister was nine months old. Theodore was twelve years old at the time. All the children had been born healthy and happy. They got along well and played together like a big, happy family. They had humble beginnings, but they made it with what they had. Tarvis could run very fast. He was also a jokester. He loved to play the game hide-and-go-seek. The other boys were kind of quiet but very industrial. They seemed to enjoy helping around the house and finding ways to make things out of mud, scraps, and rocks.

Theodore remembered how he felt as word spread about the explosion of a house. He panicked and could not move his legs when his grandmother informed him that it was his home, where his mother and siblings were. The house had exploded, and there was a big fire that burned down the entire house. Only dust and ashes remained. Theodore's mother was outside washing clothes when the explosion occurred. She was hanging clothes on the clothesline to dry in the sun when the big boom of the explosion sounded and filled the air with smoke. The only child that got out of the house was Tarvis. He managed to climb out a window. He had gotten burned and had inhaled some smoke. It was determined that faulty electrical wiring had caused the house to explode. Theodore carried guilt and pain because he was not home when it happened. He felt that he would have been able to save the rest of his siblings by getting them out of the house before it burned down. Theodore wished he could back up in time and change the way the events occurred. He just wished he could have been there to save his siblings.

Tarvis survived but not as the same Tarvis before the big explosion and fire. Tarvis suffered from mental illness. He became a person with special needs and acted similar to a Down syndrome patient. For several years, Tarvis would not talk. Yet he remained physically active. At the age of two, before the fire, he was speaking well. After the accident, his speech was impaired. Tarvis had stopped eating. He acted like he did not like food. One day, he was found eating something, but it was the soap used for bathing. His mother had gotten to him just in time before he had ingested too much of the soap. Tarvis's mother seemed very protective of him after he was injured in the accident. She survived the explosion because she was not in the house when it happened. It was unknown how Tarvis's life would progress once he grew to adult age. A special caretaker had to be with him at all times. Theodore never got over the accident. He had no closure and didn't know where the remains of his siblings were buried or if the burial ground was there where the house exploded. Every year on the anniversary of when the accident occurred, Theodore became sad and wished he knew more about exactly what happened.

Tarvis moved to the special needs center at the age of fifteen. He had some physical ailments with his legs, and there was also the speech impediment he had developed since the accident. He had a lot of speech therapy and physical therapy over the years, but the impediments remained. Tarvis found comfort and happiness when he met Mayvette at the special needs center. They later married and lived in the special needs home for active patients.

The door to the family counseling room opened. The doctor walked in to give the report on Tarvis. Tarvis was in critical condition and had congestive heart failure. He had been placed on life support. The doctor

45

directed them to the room and thought it would be good for Tarvis to visit with his family.

Theodore and Donessa opened the door to Tarvis's room. They could hear the beep of the life-support machine breathing for him. Donessa had an idea. Tarvis loved when Donessa baked her specialty and his favorite—lemon meringue pie. Every holiday, Donessa baked the pies and delivered them to the special needs home. Tarvis and Mayvette enjoyed eating the pie with their holiday dinners, and they loved sharing them with other patients that lived at the center. Donessa went to Tarvis and held his hand. She leaned over and whispered in his ear, "Tarvis, I have your lemon pie ready. Do you want to eat a slice now?"

Miraculously, Tarvis opened his eyes, smiled, and nodded his head to say, "Yes, I want the pie." Then Tarvis asked for Theodore. Theodore came to the bedside and grabbed Tarvis's hand.

Theodore said, "How about them Cowboys?" Tarvis loved football and the Dallas Cowboys. The thought of tasting the lemon pie and talking about the Cowboys seemed to bring Tarvis to full consciousness. What happened next was inconceivable to the natural human mind. Tarvis did not seem like a patient on life support. It did not seem like the Tarvis of the last forty years was speaking. There was no speech impediment, and there was no indication of a mental behavior disorder. Theodore thought he might be hallucinating and needed Donessa to witness what he was hearing. Tarvis spoke like an articulate public speaker. He seemed to exude the intelligence of a college graduate or someone with a master's or doctorate. Theodore could not understand what had happened. There was no a speech impediment. He was not bobbing his head like he usually did when he tried to speak. He just calmly and articulately delivered the speech and message.

Tarvis told Theodore everything that happened on the day of the explosion and fire. He started from the events early in the morning. Tarvis gave names and descriptions of every person that had visited the house that day. Tarvis revealed some things that brought Theodore to his knees. Donessa could hardly hold Theodore steady on his feet. Tarvis told Theodore exactly where to find his siblings. Then Tarvis began to speak with numbers. At first, Theodore thought he was trying to count; it was confusing because Tarvis had not spoken normally for forty years. Then Theodore realized that Tarvis was trying to remember and give street addresses. Tarvis gave a graveside address and other addresses. Theodore was trying to connect the dots, as this news was so unexpected.

Theodore could not fathom how a two-year-old had amassed and stored this information inside, especially with the mental behavior challenge he had suffered from after the accident. It was like a trick of the mind or an evolutionary trick. Theodore was thinking, *How could the child be a man, and then the man became the child?* Now the man was back and in a very intelligent form but on life support. It was making Theodore feel like he had gone insane. He pulled back the covers on Tarvis's bed to make sure he could see the scars from the burn and the birthmark on Tarvis's ankle. That was Tarvis's branded statement when he was born, the birthmark on his ankle in the shape of a dinosaur. Theodore was thinking that he had to be talking to a clone or robot that looked like Tarvis. When he pulled back the covers, it all matched the description of Tarvis. Tarvis was aware that Theodore was there by his bedside. He turned his head and looked at Theodore with a blank look, but it looked like he was trying to smile.

Tarvis then focused his eyes up toward the ceiling, like he was looking directly at something or someone. Tarvis said, "Theodore and Donessa, I love you very much, but I am ready to leave and go be with Mayvette." Tarvis then closed his eyes and went to sleep. Theodore and Donessa sat on the sofa in the room and hugged each other and cried. They watched as Tarvis's breathing became more and more shallow. Tarvis appeared to wake up and looked around the room, as if he was looking for Theodore and Donessa. He looked up to the ceiling and again said, "Bye, bye, bye." This happened after about two hours of shallow breathing. The monitor alarms started going off and showed that Tarvis had flatlined. It was like he knew the exact time to say bye, as if someone or something had arrived to take him somewhere. He had passed away to be with Mayvette.

Theodore had so much to do now. The message that Tarvis delivered meant Theodore needed to get a case opened to file possible criminal charges for a crime that occurred forty years ago. It was so painful and overwhelming. What had just happened? There was much work and research to be done.

Breakdown of Key Components from the Story

This is a heart-wrenching story that pulled from many of the scripts. Tarvis was born with a gift tucked inside. At the age of two, he was really a hero, even though the full extent of that was not realized until forty years later. It is almost like the events of his and Theodore's lives were destined to occur in the way it happened. This story gives meaning to the old saying, "what's done in the dark comes to the light." The *soulful* and *spiritual* scripts showed up to reveal the *intelligence*. The supernatural element creeped into this story and added scripts off the charts. *If you think you have life figured out, then you better start thinking all over again.*

The Principal

Morris Fulston had been the chief principal for the local school for twenty years and was still in charge. The school provided education for kindergarten through twelfth grade. Morris Fulston was not an ordinary principal. He had a passion for his role, and he loved the children that attended the school. He treated each student like they were his own child. He was the head principal but also like a father. Students felt comfortable confiding in him. Even when a student was referred to the office as a problem student, the situation was handled with a beneficial solution. A plan would be put in place to get the issue resolved quickly. It was a gift that belonged to Morris Fulston. He used it to benefit many children and families in the community.

If he saw the need to make a home visit to a family, he would do so. It was common to see him driving up to a house. Every parent knew that Morris Fulston would make a home visit if a problem had escalated beyond his control at the school. Most of the teachers had been trained under his tutelage to handle the majority of the problems with the elementary students. It was rare to have an extreme behavior problem.

The students, teachers, and parents all knew about the standards of the school. The cafeteria staff played a huge role in the health and nourishment of the food prepared for lunch each day. The students looked forward to the balanced, home-cooked meals that were delicious. Mrs. Brunham, the cafeteria director, planned the best meals to give energy, balance, and support for the overall physical and mental health of the students. The overall physical and mental health would also be conducive to healthy studies and learning. Mrs. Brunham planned meals such as the signature red beans and rice lunch when the football team had a game on Friday night. It was Mrs. Brunham's special recipe. She wanted them to be well nourished and with energy for the game. Her plan worked well because the football team was ranked number one in the state. It was a big team effort.

Mr. Fulston did not feel that he had done his job sufficiently if every student attending the school did not graduate and move on to the next step with a mission and success plan. He had a plan for A, B, and C students. If any student was below that level, a plan was put in place during the early elementary years of schooling. Once on track and when no other behavior or medical issue was identified, students usually mastered the levels of A, B, or C. Mr. Fulston operated like the sports scouts who navigated to find the best athletes. He found the best in each student.

It was time for the graduation and commencement exercises at the school. This was such an exciting time to celebrate the long journey from kindergarten to high school graduation. Now the fruits of the labor would accelerate as they went out to begin the next chapter of their lives. The school felt like their second home, and for some, it felt like their only home. It was time to take the next big step. It felt so good to know that each student had something planned to guide them on the way. Mr. Fulston knew the abilities of each student. He had counseled each of them, and there was a plan of action in place. From the valedictorian to the lowest C student, there was a plan. It was found that the lowest C student had an ingenious talent that awarded the potential to excel just as far or further than the A and B students.

Mr. Fulston's son was one of those students. Carter Fulston was part of the graduating class. He was not adept in the book sense or with excellent grades, but he had a unique talent for building things. He could make his own blueprint and build an entire house. At one time, he wanted to drop out of school and start building housing communities, but his father would not allow it to happen. He declared that none of his students, and certainly not his son, would become high school dropouts. Carter had continued the journey and was now graduating from high school. He was glad that his father had insisted that he stay in school. It felt like an honor to be graduating from the school under the direction of Morris Fulston. Every student felt like an honor student.

The valedictorian of the class, Clarissa Milford, was a straight-A student. She had mastered every subject. Each teacher suggested that she should go to college and major in their respective subject. The English teacher thought that Clarissa should become an English teacher or an author. The science teacher felt that it would be an injustice if Clarissa did not go into the field of science to be a scientist or to do with scientific medical practices. The math teacher declared her the best mathematician ever and thought she needed to do something in that field. The home economics teacher said that she was the perfect homemaker, cook, and seamstress. She declared unlimited possibilities, including being a famous chef with delicious recipes, created exclusively for her surfeit of different cuisines. She was very creative, taking simple ingredients and making unimaginably delicious foods with them.

Clarissa was very smart and talented, but she lacked self-confidence. She was a stutterer and was overweight. She felt so unattractive. Even though Clarissa had the stuttering issue and sometimes it took a while to get the words out, she was still a class favorite. Most people found comfort in going to her to be the ear or sounding board to listen to their relationship problems. Clarissa felt nonthreatening and nonjudgmental, and people found it easy to talk to her. Clarissa was very capable of giving sound and worthwhile advice. She made people smile.

Mr. Fulston knew that he had to find a way to get a scholarship for Clarissa. He was aware of Clarissa's family situation. Clarissa's mother had a tenth-grade education, and her father had a fourth-grade education. Clarissa's mother did not work, and her father did small jobs in construction that did not provide a continuous flow of income. Mr. Fulston used his ability to network with his contacts to find a program that provided full scholarships, including books, room and board, and spending money, for students who suffered some type of disability or indisposition. It was part of the Rehabilitation Boost, a local program. Stuttering qualified as one of the ailments for the full scholarship. Mr. Fulston took Clarissa to the office to apply for the scholarship. The scholarship was granted and approved. Clarissa graduated with a full scholarship to go to any college of her choice. Clarissa and her family were so appreciative of what Mr. Fulston had done. He worked hard to assure that his students were prepared for success after graduation. He knew that he had to work something out in a grand way for the valedictorian of the class. Clarissa was a fine gem waiting to be discovered.

Carter Fulston started his own construction and housing business. One of Carter's visions was to bring some affordable housing to the community, as most of the community was impoverished. Carter's designs were economical and perfect for the needs of the community. When construction was underway, Carter hired Clarissa's father to be the handyman. Clarissa was very appreciative because the job brought a steady income for her father. Carter always had another project waiting as one got completed. Carter's niche was perfect for the business and his visions. He inherited the gift of maturation for the cause, just as his father had done as the principal of the school for so many years. Carter was now doing the same thing, helping every community to succeed with affordable housing. He was building in many other towns and cities across the state.

Clarissa had gone to college and excelled, just as everyone expected. She had decided to major in accounting and minor in psychology. Clarissa had taken counseling. The scholarship with the Rehabilitation Boost Program was a perfect match for Clarissa. She had lost weight while in college, and the speech impediment was hardly noticeable. The program also came with funding for counseling or medical aid, depending on the indisposition of each student. The stuttering was caused by the situation at home. Clarissa worried about the family finances. She had awakened many mornings to hear arguing between her parents about the problems, and it had shattered Clarissa's emotions.

She shut down and did not talk about it but just concentrated on her studies. When she tried to think about the situation in her mind and communicate her thoughts, it was so painful that words would not flow. The counseling that Clarissa had inspired her to pick psychology as a minor. She wanted to major in accounting because she wanted to be sure that she would be a master at handling the finances for her family. She wanted to make extinct the problems that had weakened her family. Clarissa graduated from college with high honors.

Clarissa had been placed in a really good job. The college recruiting and placement center had a good program to match students with jobs. Clarissa was a good match for the position in general accounting management. She accepted the job and excelled quickly. She was promoted to assistant controller and was doing well. A magazine had come to the company and interviewed her as one the top one hundred women in the country most likely to succeed. Clarissa had come a long way. The words "it really does take a village to raise and help the children succeed" were so true for the students in the community.

Mr. Fulston's efforts were monumental and historical. Many students felt that they owed so much to him, but according to him, they owed him nothing. His reward was seeing his students succeed.

Clarissa had come home to visit her parents for the weekend. She also had come to see Mr. Fulston. After twenty-five years of service at the school and in the community, Mr. Fulston had recently retired because of illness. For quite a while, he had not been able to turn his neck without pain. It felt like a crook was in his neck that could not be straightened.

It had also gotten to the point where he could not look in the rearview mirror when driving. He finally realized that he needed to seek medical attention. It was not good news. He was diagnosed with a terminal stage of cancer. Before the diagnosis, Mr. Fulston had been on Carter about settling down, finding a good wife, and starting his own family. Carter was a shaker and mover just like his father. They both enjoyed their lines of work, and they both took it to heart.

There's another piece to this story. Carter had been keeping it a secret—his plans to settle down and start his family. Carter had not let his dad know that he had a girlfriend and was planning on asking her to marry him. Carter stayed so busy on the road, building homes, and he had advanced to building other commercial structures. He had done designs for tall buildings in large cities. He was so busy on the road, and he knew it would take a special woman to understand him, stick by his side, and visualize his visions. It had to be an unselfish woman who was smart and easy to talk to. Carter had done some work repairing some of the dormitories at the college where Clarissa attended. He saw her and how good she looked. He could hardly believe it was the same Clarissa from his hometown. She had lost weight, was very articulate, and was of course very intelligent. Carter thought, *If this is what going to college does, then everyone should attend.* He wondered if there was a fountain of youth somewhere that came with the curriculum. Clarissa looked so good, but of course, the beauty was shining from inside out. She was beautiful to Carter even when she was overweight in high school. He did not approach her then because he felt that he would be teased by his buddies. Now that he had found himself and could see clearly his visions, he knew what he wanted. He started dating Clarissa when she was a junior in college. It was right after he finished working on the dormitories at the college. Carter was a prime contractor and was highly sought out for many projects across the state. They had been having a long-distance relationship, but they visited each other often and stayed in touch daily.

Clarissa had come home for the weekend, and she and Carter had decided it was time to make the announcement to Mr. Fulston and to Clarissa's family. Clarissa was so excited about planning the wedding because she wanted to prepare some of her delicious recipes for the reception. Carter wanted it to be outside because he wanted to design a heavenly type of display setting. He envisioned Clarissa walking up the aisle paved with gold to meet him as he stood at the pearly gates to welcome his bride to a life that he vowed to make feel like heaven on earth. He knew he had chosen the best woman for him and felt so blessed that fate had brought them together. He wanted it to be like something never seen before. He then envisioned adding another element to his construction business. He could build spectacular wedding scenes for people across the world.

Carter felt nervous yet excited to break the news to his Father. Carter did not know what the feeling inside him was. He felt kind of like he was going to propose to Clarissa again. This was his father though, and it was exciting news because his father was very fond of Clarissa. Carter and Clarissa walked in the room smiling and holding hands. Carter said, "Dad, let me introduce you to my beautiful future wife, Ms. Clarissa Milford, soon to be Mrs. Clarissa Fulston."

Spontaneously and at the same time, Carter and Clarissa said, "We love each other very much and want to spend the rest of our lives together." It was a synchronous moment that felt blissful and perfect.

Mr. Fulston was so ecstatically happy with the news. He felt that he could not have picked a better daughter-in-law than Clarissa. Clarissa had always felt like a daughter to him anyway. Mr. Fulston wanted to get out of bed and hug them, but he was coughing profusely and was very weak. He told them how much he loved them and how happy it made him to know that they would be happy with a good life. Mr. Fulston told Clarissa that he could not wait to hold his grandchild. He told Carter and Clarissa that he would be at the wedding even if he had to come in his rolling bed.

Carter and Clarissa left his father's house to start the wedding plans. As they were talking, Carter was thinking about the look in his father's eyes when he said that he could not wait to hold his grandchild. He asked Clarissa if maybe they should have the wedding as soon as possible. Clarissa told Carter that she felt it was a good idea to have the wedding as soon as possible because his father seemed very weak. Clarissa also let Carter know that she had missed her cycle and a pregnancy-testing kit had been positive. Clarissa wondered if Carter's father already knew that. It was hard to get anything past him. He was the type of principal that knew it before you knew it. He had that deep type of intuition. Carter hugged and kissed Clarissa and said, "Yes, baby, this is the way it was meant to be. This is great news, and we will marry as soon as possible."

Clarissa said, "But it will take time to plan the big wedding that we envisioned."

Carter said, "Yes, we can get married with a small wedding and have the big wedding later. It can be next year for our first anniversary. As creative as you and I are together, we can do it any way we want to, and it will be beautiful because this how we do it, baby! With you by my side, I feel that everything is possible. That is why I want to have the wedding feel like what people have imagined heaven to be."

Carter got the call that his father had been rushed to the hospital. He and Clarissa made it to the hospital soon after Mr. Fulston had been admitted. It was apparent that Mr. Fulston was very sick and in the last stage of life. However, he was still glad to see his son, and he asked about Clarissa. Mr. Fulston really loved Clarissa, and Carter loved her too. Carter and Clarissa discussed a plan of action. They decided to get married right way in the chapel in the hospital. Carter was praying that enough time would be granted for them to get it set up. Carter and Carissa left the hospital to get the marriage license. They asked Reverend Wells, the local pastor, to marry them.

Father time cooperated, and the private wedding happened. The medical staff rolled Mr. Fulston's bed to the chapel, and he witnessed the union of Carter and Clarissa. As they were pronounced husband and wife, Carter kissed his beautiful wife. Something felt heavenly. It felt surreal to Carter and Clarissa. They could hear Mr. Fulston trying to say something, but it sounded like a whisper. It even sounded like they heard a weak clap or applause. Carter and Clarissa were spellbound, staring at each other like they had been sprinkled with fairy tale dust.

They were so caught up in the moment that they did not realize that the medical staff had rushed Mr. Fulston out of the chapel. They went to exit the chapel and wondered when the nurse had taken Mr. Fulston back to his room. They happily walked, holding hands, to Mr. Fulston's room. Carter and Carissa were met by the chaplain and Mr. Fulston's main nurse as they walked down the hallway.

The nurse informed them that Mr. Fulston had passed away but not before he witnessed the union joining them as husband and wife. It must have occurred during the moment that Carter and Clarissa felt frozen in some type of enchanted time zone, as they stared at each other like frozen statues, hypnotized by the matrimony. Carter felt that as he and Clarissa were hypnotized in the bliss of love, his father was separating and granting the blessings to his son, new daughter, and his grandchild on the way. The nurse informed them that he had a smile on his face and was at peace. The nurse did confirm that he had tried to clap after the minister had pronounced them husband and wife. She said that his face looked enamored with a glow of a radiant candle light. It was unbelievable the way the events occurred, but leave it to Morris Fulston with his big soul to go out in a spectacular way. Carter wanted more than ever to plan the big heavenly wedding.

Nine months later, Carter and Clarissa became the proud parents of a set of twins. Cartressa and Cartelle Fulston, a boy and a girl, were delivered happy and healthy. Both screamed loudly to the world, "We are here." Carter wished Mr. Fulston could have been alive and well to witness the moment. They both would always tell the stories about what Mr. Fulston accomplished and contributed to society.

So much had happened during the first year with the loss of Mr. Fulston. Mr. Fulston was well known for his contributions to the school and community. His going-home celebration was huge. Events and festivities were planned for an entire week before the final burial. So many wanted to give tributes to Mr. Fulston in their own special way. Many programs were planned.

Clarissa had to get through the pregnancy, which was an adjustment. Carter and Clarissa continued to work their jobs. Also, Clarissa was Carter's main accountant with the business. She reviewed all the ledgers even though he had some accountants on staff.

They decided to wait and do the second wedding on their third anniversary. The twins were big enough to participate in the wedding party. It was even more spectacular than previously imagined. Carter had designed a setting that seemed impossible for any human to conceive. It was breathtaking. People from the local community and other towns came to witness the event of the year. It was also a way for potential clients to see Carter's spectacular designs. It felt like Mr. Fulston was part of the wedding party. Carter had designed a life-size statue of Mr. Fulston, and it had automatic wheels and a remote that made it appear as if he was walking in, part of the wedding party. The crowd gasped when Mr. Fulston came strolling down the aisle waving, just as he did at the school each day. If you were fortunate enough to get an invitation to the wedding, you left with fortune-filled eyes from witnessing something grand and amazing. It gave the feeling that a miracle had been granted to everyone there. It was a big family celebration, and everyone was getting a taste of heaven.

The twins were so excited. It felt like they got to meet their grandfather. Even though he passed away before they were born, Carter and Clarissa had told them a lot about him and showed them pictures. It felt like they knew their grandfather. Spiritually, they could feel him inside of them.

The wedding was simply beautiful. More words needed to be added to the dictionary to describe what Carter and Clarissa rolled out for their third anniversary. It was ineffable to try to describe the scene with words. It was an inspiration and gift for themselves and the many guests that were fortunate enough to attend. Clarissa's specialty cuisines were savory, delicious, and exquisite. People were heard murmuring that they had never tasted anything so good before, while devouring every morsel on their plates.

Breakdown of Key Components from the Story

From the deep and *compassionate* soul of Morris Fulston, something big was started with his contributions to the community. He used many of the scripts to power the education system that he directed for so many years. He was *determined, generous,* and very *influential.* His success was heightened with the success of the many students who graduated and started their own lives. The scripts from the sounding board were used by so many people as they realized their own worth, and their potential was defined by one of the greatest masters, Morris Fulston. It makes it easy to envision the Morris Fulston Foundation that was built to help many people and causes. It is incredible when the gifts are granted, opened, and used to fulfill a wonderful lifetime. The genuine contributions and leadership of a soul can live forever. *The bright light of the soul can shine for many generations to come.*

The Call from Beyond

It was a bright, sunny Wednesday morning. The phone rang loudly. Annanda thought she was hearing the doorbell ring. Her mind was playing tricks on her as she lay in bed trying to sleep, while others were out enjoying the bright sunshine. That was the nature of the beast though, for the workers so fortunate—or maybe unfortunate—to work the graveyard shift. Midnight to eight in the morning was Annanda's shift. If she did not get home and get a nap right away, the nap would not happen, because soon it would be time to pick up Theron from day care. Theron, Annanda and Delton's three-year-old son, hated to see his mother leave in the middle of the night to go to work. The fact was that the midnight hour arrived so quickly to start the process all over again, back to work. It just seemed to shorten the day. Annanda thought about the grind and the goals that she and her husband, Delton, had envisioned. Annanda wondered if she and Delton had been too opportunistic with their visions. Annanda had a good job that she continued to work, while Delton had quit his job to venture into a start-up business. The midnight shift paid a shift differential, which was added income. They thought that if they worked hard together early, while still in their twenties, maybe they could retire in their forties and travel the world.

Annanda rolled over to look at caller ID and saw that it was Delton calling. He had finished his shift at the business, and the employee he had hired and trained would cover the day shift until he got back to close in the evening from 6:00 p.m. to 12:00 a.m. Delton seemed to be doing a really good job learning the operation and food preparation.

Delton and Annanda had used their 401(k) savings to purchase the sandwich and coffee shop. The savings wasn't enough, so they also had to get a bank loan. They had purchased it from another young couple that moved away to another country. It was a big risk, and Delton's nerves were shaking each day because the business was taking off so slowly. The only income was from Annanda's job. Delton was calling to let Annanda know that he would be home soon, in about fifteen minutes, to relax and get some rest before it was six o'clock and he had to go back to the business. He thought at least he could get a good four-hour nap.

The grind was turning out to be very grinding. Some things turn out to be harder to accomplish than how they appear when conceived in the mind. Delton was nervous but still felt young and energetic and was hopeful that he would have the business up and going, with sales and customers increasing every day. Delton told Annanda that he would be home in about fifteen minutes. Annanda said, "Okay, babe. See you soon. I love you."

Annanda hung up the phone, and it started ringing again like it does when someone is still on the other line. Annanda thought, *Why is Delton calling back? He said he would be home soon.* Annanda answered the phone saying, "Hello!" She was about to say, "What else is it, Delton? I just talked to you." The voice on the other line startled her, and she was in disbelief. She then realized that she must have been asleep, and Delton had not called her. She must have been dreaming that Delton called. Delton was probably still working.

The voice on the other line said, "Hey, Annanda."

Annanda replied, "Mama?"

"Yes, Annanda. I am sorry to bother you, but I need your help. I did not want to bother the other children because I knew it would scare them. I knew I would not scare you."

Annanda said, "Okay, Mama." Annanda was sitting up, shaking in disbelief, because her mother had passed away seventeen months earlier. The previous year in May, she and her seven siblings had laid their beautiful and courageous mother to rest after a long battle with cancer.

Annanda's mother continued to talk, and Annanda could hear a lot of people talking and laughing in the background. Annanda asked, "Mama, who are all those people that I hear talking in the background?" It sounded like they were having a party or something. Annanda heard her mother say three different names of people talking in the background. Annanda was so caught up in the surprise call that she did not remember the names.

Her mother said that she also had a new name. She said, "They call me Precious now." On earth, she was Annestha. She went on to ask Annanda to please help Kingston. Kingston was the baby of the family, Annanda's baby brother. Annanda's mother informed her that he was suffering financially and needed some money to buy food. Kingston still lived in the house just steps from where his mother lived when she was alive. Annanda's mother, Annestha, was the head of the family, the rock and backbone. Her love and compassion for her children reached no boundaries when she was alive and well. Annanda's mother asked her to please wire Kingston some money as soon as possible. She said that she would find a way to get it back to her, to pay her back soon. She just needed her to help Kingston today.

Annanda said, "Okay. Sure, Mama."

Then Annanda's mother started asking her to repeat after her. It was some type of coded language that Annanda did not understand, but she was trying to follow it. Annanda's mother said, "I am giving you this code because the day will come for you to use it."

Annanda said, "Okay, Mama. I love and miss you so much." Annanda thought she heard the sound of the alarm going off. Her mother must have hung up the phone. Annanda started begging for her mother to please not hang up. She wanted to talk to her mother for as long as possible because it just did not seem real that she was fortunate enough to have her mother trust her with the request from heaven.

Annanda was sitting in the bed with the telephone receiver in her hand when Delton walked in the room, kissed her, and said, "See? I told you I would be home in about fifteen minutes." He saw the expression on Annanda's face and asked, "What's wrong?"

Annanda asked him if she sounded like she was asleep when he called earlier. Delton said, "No, you were not asleep. We talked for about five minutes." Annanda told him about the call that she had just received on the telephone. She told him that she thought it was him calling her right back. Delton just hugged her and said, "Oh, baby, you probably imagined that because you are still grieving over the loss of your beautiful mother. She was very precious, and I love and miss her too."

Annanda said, "How do you know about Precious?"

Delton looked confused and said, "You just need to get some rest. Those night shifts can be very taxing on the mind and body." Delton kissed her on the forehead and went to the kitchen to get something to snack on and to sit and watch a little television. He usually took his nap while sitting in the recliner in front of the television. Annanda knew that she was not imagining that call because the conversation was very clear and with a request. She also thought that for Delton to describe her mother as precious was an indication given from beyond that connected to the conversation with her mother.

Annanda decided to call her oldest sister, who lived in the same town where Kingston lived and her mother had lived. Annanda's sister confirmed that Kingston was having some problems and had taken on another job. Annanda's sister told her that Kingston had come by the night before and had eaten supper at her house. Annanda informed her sister why she was calling and inquiring about Kingston. When Annanda finished updating her sister about the call from their mother, Annanda's sister believed in her heart that the call had happened.

She screamed out a shout of "Hallelujah!" She said that she could still feel the strength of their mother guiding her from day to day. This conversation with Annanda confirmed her belief that the light of the spirit never dies.

Annanda did exactly as her mother requested. She wired Kingston enough money to help him get through the next couple of weeks. Annanda did not think about getting any sleep before the midnight hour arrived. She felt so full of energy and did not feel sleepy. That call from beyond with her mother had lit a fire inside her soul. She felt like she was invincible. It felt like her stomach had been washed from inside out with soap. It felt so clean and pure. It was a feeling she had not felt before. She could not wait to get to work and perform her duties, as she felt that some type of breakthrough had come through from heaven.

On Friday night, Delton called from the business. He said that something unbelievable had happened. The business had taken off in a big way. He said that he had to close early because everything in the shop had been sold. There was no inventory to make any orders. He said that he was going to have to call and see if he could get an emergency order delivered.

Annanda knew where all the customers were coming from. It was her mother directing and guiding them in. She was taking care of things from heaven, just like the mother she always was. She kept the family going by finding a way to make something big out of what seemed like nothing. Now she was still doing it large and in charge.

Annanda still had the feeling of being invincible. She thought about the day when her mother called. Annanda made a vow that she was going to turn up the switch on her own light to shine brighter. Annanda was thinking about her mother's love and compassion for the family and her children. Annanda decided that the business would be run like a closely knit family, and they would spread the love inside the business so the customers would feel it as soon they walked through the door.

The business kept growing and expanded to six locations. Annanda had to take a leave from her job to help Delton with the business, as her administrative expertise was needed due to the rapid growth. Annanda could see a bright future and felt that they would be able to retire in their forties, just like they had envisioned, if the success and growth continued. Annanda felt within her heart and soul that she had the support and protection of her mother watching and helping from heaven.

Breakdown of Key Components from the Story

What a powerful story and message this brought into being that pulled scripts from the supernatural! Annanda and Delton used the scripts of *adventure, determination, organization, intelligence,* and *vision,* and many others showed up for them to answer the call to the growing and expanding business. The testimonial of this story brings reason to believe that the scripts or inside coding in each person is also powered by the light glimmering inside, waiting to be turned up to higher beams. When that occurs, the greatest gift has been granted and delivered. *A vision may be the reflection of a path from a previous life.*

The Rollover—It's Over

Vivian Knewford was filled with excitement as she started packing her bags and gifts to take home for Christmas. It was the first Christmas in more than five years that she would get to spend with her family back down south. It had been six years since she had last seen her family. She had gone home for her mother's funeral. That was the saddest and biggest wound that Vivian had ever felt, saying goodbye to her mother. Vivian avoided going back home because it was too sad thinking that her mother would not be standing on the porch to give her that huge, loving hug. The only saving grace that she could attach to the sadness was that it took her mind off the problems with her abusive husband. Nothing seemed worse than the pain of losing her mother.

Vivian made a vow to herself that she was going to turn off the madness being dealt by Terrance Smuthers, her abusive husband of twenty-three years. Somehow, she had managed the problems with his abuse so that her family down south never really knew the full extent of what she was going through. She, at times, had called and confided in her sister, Jerrica. It was when she was at her lowest. Terrance had gotten his car impounded for parking in a fire zone. He was too trifling to pay to get his car from the impound. He asked Vivian to go and get it. He always did harmful things like that. He had so many parking tickets, and they did not hurt him. The tickets were billed to Vivian because the car was in her name. He took Vivian's car keys to use her car to go to see one of his lovers. When Vivian tried to stop him, he punched her with his fist. Vivian was left home wounded, stranded, and soaked with tears in the cold, windy city. That was the night the breakthrough came into her mind, and she made the decision that it would be over.

She had finally made good on that vow. She had filed for divorce, and it had become final in March, nine months before her Christmas vacation. Terrence did not contest it, as he did not even show up for the court hearing. He probably did not believe that Vivian was going to go through with it. That was just the way Terrance handled things. He was irresponsible, uncaring, and entitled, as if the world revolved around him and his good looks. He had so many different women that he was playing it was hard to see how he kept up with all the mischief. Vivian felt that a shift had taken place when she made the subtle change within herself that she just did not care anymore. She could tell that Terrance could see that he no longer had the upper hand with her. She could see that he was uncomfortable, and that discomfort somehow had stopped him from being abusive. Vivian noticed that he was staying away for days at a time, and when he came face-to-face with her, he seemed nervous. The Terrence before feared nothing and acted as if he had nerves made of steal. He was also very polite and on his best behavior. He acted like he was trying to get his life together with one of his other women. He had finally moved out of the apartment with Vivian and was living somewhere else, probably with one of his women. He had moved out in June, three months after the divorce was final. Vivian was relieved that Terrence was finally out of her life. She could now move on peacefully. Vivian hoped that Terrence would finally grow up to be a better man with whoever he was with.

Vivian could not wait to see her family now that she was free of Terrance and his abuse. She was proud of the stand she had taken and the woman she had become. Her mother's death was an eye-opener that life does not go on forever in the physical sense of each individual person. It is important to take your life back and make the best of it. Jerrica, Vivian's sister, had recently had a baby boy, and Vivian wanted to get there just in time for his first birthday party. Vivian could not wait to see her nephew.

Terrance had stopped by the night before. He said that he was just thinking about her and wanted to see how she was doing. He was hungry and told Vivian that he missed her cooking. Vivian was a great cook. Terrance once told her that he believed she could boil a dirty rock and make it taste like a scrumptious delicacy. Vivian had just finished eating supper and had some leftovers. Terrance went into the kitchen and helped himself. That was the way Terrance was—bold and unashamed to help himself to whatever was available. He often bragged about what a great jock he was and how nothing could embarrass him. Bowling was his favorite sport. He also lifted weights and was super vain about his body and muscles. He used to say to Vivian, "Look at these big thunderbolts here. I can rip any man apart with these things." Terrance was very violent and with a quick temper. He had lost his last job because he punched his boss in the face and left him on the floor unconscious.

He saw Vivian's bags packed and asked her if she was going somewhere. She said, "Yes, Terrance, I am going home for Christmas."

He smiled and said, "Oh that's great. I will drive you to the airport. That way you don't have to catch a cab or leave your car at the airport and pay for parking. You can just leave your car here, and I will come by and check on it while you are gone. I have a new car of my own now," he said. Vivian looked out the window and saw that he was driving a Geo Tracker. It was a very small sports utility vehicle. Vivian hesitantly said okay, but it felt like she should not have agreed to let him take her to the airport. She wondered if it was just a way for him to try to get back in and have access to all the undeserved perks he was accustomed to getting when they were married. He thanked her for the meal and said that he would be by the next morning at seven o'clock sharp.

The morning came, and Terrance showed up on time, ready to take Vivian to the airport. Vivian noticed that he had dark circles under his eyes. She asked him if he had gotten enough sleep last night. He told her that he was just having problems with allergies because he lived in an apartment that had recently been painted. Whether that story was true or not was unknown, as Terrance had a way of making up lies right on the spot, whenever he felt the need to. Terrance also said that he was doing well and had gotten a new job up by the airport. Vivian did not know whether to believe that or not because he had not attempted to find work for the last year that he was living with her. He just continued to mooch off her income.

When they first got into the little Tracker, Terrance asked for Vivian's house keys. Vivian asked, "Why do you need to get the keys if you have a new apartment?" He begged her for the keys, using the reason that if the fresh paint continued to make him sick, he would not be able to start the new job, which was very important to him. He said that he was trying to come up to reach her level and did not want to lose the good job he had just started. Kindhearted Vivian hesitantly agreed.

As the drive to the airport continued, Terrance became very quiet and still. Vivian asked him if something was wrong. He said, "You were such a romantic, Vivian. You wanted it all and blamed me for not being able to give you the life of your dreams."

Vivian replied, "Well, that is behind us now, Terrance, and I am not blaming you for anything. You have your own life now, and it appears that you are doing well, and I am so proud of you." Vivian noticed that Terrance's eyes had turned red, and they looked strained.

Terrance asked, "So are you going home to tell your family that I am nothing but a rotten egg?"

Vivian said, "Well, no, I had not planned on doing that. I am just looking forward to enjoying Christmas with my family and meeting my new nephew, Jerrica's son. He is celebrating his first birthday today, and the plane will land just in time to get to the party."

Terrance then said, "Oh no, I need to give you what you want in a romantic way. We are not going to the airport! It is time for romance for the romantic. We are going to elope, and you will love me again like you did when you first married me!"

Terrance turned the stirring wheel of the little Tracker, and things went blank. The Tracker flipped over several times and landed in a grassy field right off the interstate, a little before the exit to the airport. It happened so fast. There was no evidence of anything that could have caused the accident. Vivian just remembered saying to her inner spirituality and guidance system and to God, "Protect me."

She then heard the answer, "You will be safe, but not sure about Terrance." When she opened her eyes, the truck was upside down. She realized that God had answered. Vivian felt that she had witnessed the meaning of GOD—Granted On Delivery. She had been granted the delivery into this world, and God had delivered again by protecting her in this accident. This was like receiving a gift that got opened in a huge way. It is like a gift that floats around the world for anyone to grab on to by just asking. She was conscious and coherent, but she needed to figure out how to get her purse and airplane ticket. She saw that her ticket had fallen out of her purse on the ground under the Tracker. Somehow Vivian managed to kick the door open, and she jumped out to the ground. She picked up her purse and the airline ticket. She heard the sound of sirens. She then looked and saw a large rodent running through the grass. She was so glad that she did not see that before she decided to kick the door open and jump out. The sight of that thing might have made her decide to just stay inside, turned upside down.

Vivian finally had the thought, Oh, *I better try and help Terrance get out.* By that time, the fire department and ambulance had arrived. Someone driving by must have seen the accident. Vivian did not get a chance to see if Terrance was okay. The vehicle was turned upside down, and when she got out of the car, she did not even see Terrance in the car. She wondered if Terrance had gotten thrown from the car. Vivian did not know what happened. The Tracker just started rolling over and over. It did not seem like Terrance had swerved the Tracker to make it flip over. Possibly it was the energy that took over when Terrance made the decision that he was not going to the airport. It was a mysterious accident.

The police officer said, "Ma'am, are you okay?"

Vivian replied, "Yes, I feel fine." He asked if she was in the Tracker when it flipped over. Vivian said, "Yes I was." She wondered why he was asking her a question like that. He asked her to come and sit inside the fire truck. As she walked to the fire truck, she looked back at the little Tracker and realized why. It was unbelievable that she had been in the Tracker. The pieces of the little truck scattered everywhere looked no bigger that Vivian's entire body. Vivian could not see how she was able to kick the door open and get out. The ambulance had already taken Terrance to the hospital. She looked on the ground and saw Terrance's bowling ball and one of his hand weights.

Vivian proceeded to give the report to the police officer. The officer suggested that she go in the ambulance to the hospital to get checked out. Vivian noticed that the officer had checked the box on the accident report form that marked the wreck as causing a fatality. Vivian thought, *Surely that does not mean what I am thinking it means.* It was hard to believe that Terrance was fatally injured and she was alive and well. Vivian arrived at the hospital to get checked out. Vivian's vitals were fine. The doctor just told her they would run more tests and start an intravenous drip to rebuild her fluids. She was slightly dehydrated and swollen from the trauma. She asked about Terrance and was informed that the next of kin had been contacted and would stop by to give her the status. Vivian thought that they probably contacted Terrance's father, or maybe they called his new lady that he lived with.

Finally, the news came in about Terrance. Terrance's father walked into Vivian's room to see how she was doing. He informed her that Terrance was deceased. He had arrived at the hospital DOA (dead on arrival). He informed Vivian that Terrance had a severe crush to his head, and his liver was split in half. Vivian wondered if the impact of the rollover had caused the bowling ball or the weights to crush Terrance's head. Vivian thought about the rat running across the field like it had come from under the wreckage. She wondered if it represented Terrance's last life or soul. Vivian had suspected that Terrance may not have survived when she saw the fatality box checked on the accident report; however, it was hard to believe that Terrance was gone for good. Terrance always appeared larger than life, and nothing could stop him. It was just so hard to believe. Vivian gave Terrance's father her condolences, and she felt kind of sad yet relieved.

Terrance's father informed Vivian that Lavoria Jenkins was there at the hospital. She was called because she was the owner of the Geo Tracker that Terrance was driving. Vivian started talking and reflecting about Terrance. His father immediately interrupted and said, "None of that matters now, Vivian. It is all over, and Terrance is no longer your worry." Vivian felt kind of sad for Terrance and the life he thought he owned forever. Vivian thanked God for protecting her. Was the accident also a way of protecting her from what Terrance was about to force her to do? He had said that they would not be going to the airport but would elope and get married again. Terrance must not have been happy with Lavoria Jenkins, or he did not feel secure with her. Terrance had gotten used to the security and kindness that Vivian always delivered, no matter what the circumstance.

Vivian asked the nurse to assist her with contacting her family to let them know she was not on the plane that would be arriving at the airport, due to the accident. When Vivian called to tell Jerrica about what had happened, Jerrica could not believe the news. That was some news just before Christmas. The terror of Terrance Smuthers was finally over. The story of how it all happened was so dramatic, like right out of a novel. It just did not seem real. Jerrica felt so blessed that Vivian survived the accident and would be okay.

Vivian was discharged from the hospital on the second day. The accident had occurred on Sunday, and Vivian was discharged on Tuesday. Jerrica had rescheduled Vivian's travel arrangements to leave on Tuesday after Vivian checked out of the hospital. Vivian had missed the birthday party on Sunday, but she would make it home in time for Christmas.

Vivian made the flight, and it landed safely. Jerrica went to the airport to get Vivian. She could not wait to hear all the details about the accident and everything that had happened leading up to it. Life would be changing now for the better, and she hoped that Vivian would make the decision to move back home. This would be a beautiful Christmas for rekindling and rebuilding. Jerrica would do everything possible to help Vivian get through this and finally move forward with a good life. The rest of the family was waiting to join in to give the big family love and hugs that the Knewfords were famous for rendering.

Breakdown of Key Components from the Story

Now this story is one that used many of the scripts. Vivian had been sustained by using the scripts for a long time through thick and thin. The scripts sheltered her during the time of storm and protected her during the accident with her belief and *spirituality* circling all around on the scene. Another miracle got delivered right before the holiday season. Terrance had tapped into the sounding board also and used the scripts to hang on to keep playing his games, but he got caught in his own shadows. There is so much to be learned by this story. Vivian remained *strong* to the vows that she had made for a long time, but Terrance caused them to sever. Vivian's script and her character reigned superior over the darkness that lurked all around. The delivery showed up again. *The rollover can be the turnover that delivers the turnaround and a new set of keys.*

The Bond of a Lifetime

Rivera Munson sat in the chair making flowers for her granddaughter Rivenna.

It was homecoming, and Rivenna was the ninth-grade homecoming queen for the homecoming court. Rivenna was so excited, and her grandmother really wanted to do a good job designing the flowers and other decorations for Rivenna's float. It made Rivera feel like a young girl again as she reflected back to when she too was elected the ninth-grade queen. She was also voted the tenth-grade queen the next year. Those were such golden and carefree days in preparation for the adult life where the simple fun and joy seemed to run away quickly.

Rivera started thinking about the road not taken. She was thinking about Solomon Craven. She had finished the most beautiful bouquet for Rivenna's float and then dipped back into the time travel of her mind. Rivera had gone to a basketball game that was in another town against the school's rival. It was so much fun to ride the school bus to a game and not to school. Something felt magical about getting away in the evening and during nightfall. On the way back from the game, Rivera took the seat next to Solomon Craven. It appeared to make Solomon uncomfortable, as he just turned his head and looked out the window. Some of the school's most flirtatious guys got on the bus and kept teasing Solomon. They were saying things like, "Now how did you get so lucky to get that seat, Solomon?" "What I would not give to trade seats with you, Solomon." "Solomon, do you know what to do with all of that sitting next to you?" Solomon just continued to stare out the window quietly. The teasing and meddling got worse when Jeremy Brackins said, "Oh, I know what's wrong, Solomon. You don't want to look at Rivera because you don't want her to see that big scar on the side of your face. Look, Solomon Scarface, don't be afraid. I won't hurt you. Just give up your seat. Scar!"

That was when Rivera finally said, "Stop it, guys. That is enough and so unkind and definitely not representative of our team spirit for this school."

Looking shocked, Jeremy said, "Okay. Sorry!" He did not want Rivera upset with him, so he went to the back of the bus and found a seat. She apologized to Solomon, and he just quietly and sadly nodded his head as a gesture of saying thank you. She felt sorry for Solomon. Solomon had an accident riding his bicycle down a steep hill near his home. He ran into a pole and was found unconscious with a large cut on his forehead and the side of his face. He was out of school for a month. Rivera sat next to him because she was so glad to see him back at school and trying to get back into the swing of things again. She was surprised that he had decided to go to the game. He was quiet all the way back to the school, and they both exited the bus to find their parents waiting to pick them up.

The next week, Solomon moved away to another state to live with his mother. He had been living with his grandparents. When Rivera heard the news, she thought, *Well, at least Solomon does not have to face the teasing and bullying that has been taking place at school.* Maybe he could meet new friends, ones who were kind and not judgmental about what had happened to his face. It could be a new beginning for him. Solomon was two years older than Rivera. Rivera felt in her heart that Solomon would soon discover his worth and gain confidence once he moved to a new environment. Rivera and Solomon kept in touch by writing and sending a postcard at least once a month.

It was Christmas of the next year. Rivera was now in tenth grade and thinking about the upcoming college life. She had enough credits to graduate early. She just needed to take two classes during the summer, and she could skip the eleventh grade and go right into her senior year. But for now, she wanted to enjoy the Christmas break and have fun with her family.

She looked out the window and noticed the classiest-looking white sports car drive into the driveway. She wondered, *Who could that be? I have not seen a car like that in town before.* She then noticed the license plates were from a different state. Then the door opened, and there stood the most elegant-looking man, dressed in a white suit. He looked tall and distinguished, and she did not recognize him. He came up to the porch and up the steps to the door and knocked. Rivera immediately opened the door, and to her surprise, it was Solomon. A transformation had taken place since she had last seen him. He had grown several inches and was very handsome. His hair was very long, and it was becoming to his facial structure. He used to wear his hair cut very short. He even spoke so confidently, with a deep voice. "Hello, Rivera, it is so good to see you again, and what a pleasure for me this moment has gifted."

Rivera thought, *Oh my goodness. Is this the same person?* She welcomed him inside to sit down. He had brought her a Christmas gift, a box of chocolates and a bottle of perfume. He asked Rivera's mother if it would be okay to take Rivera for a ride into town and by the school. He just wanted to get out and revisit his past surroundings and think about how he had changed and to see if his memory of the town had changed. Thankfully, Rivera's mother said yes.

Rivera felt so special sitting next to him in the fancy sports car. She knew that they would be the talk of the town if someone spotted that car driving around. It would get a lot of attention. People would want to find out who was in that car and what was going on. Solomon deserved to get positive attention after what he had gone thorough when he lived in the town just a few years back. Rivera and Solomon rode around and talked. They caught up on things and found that they had much in common with their beliefs and philosophies about life and the future. He felt like a good friend that could be a future business partner or something.

Christmas was so much fun, and the gift of Solomon showing up had been unexpected. They agreed to stay in touch, and he planned to be back for the summer. Rivera enjoyed spending time with him. She liked him as a good friend.

The next summer came, and Solomon decided to spend it back at his grandparents' house. He wanted to spend as much time as possible with Rivera. Rivera realized that possibly she had a shallow or selfish side because she was disappointed that he came back to town on the bus and not in the fancy sports car. The sports car belonged to his mother. He had it during the Christmas holidays because his mother had let him use the car. Solomon planned to stay the entire summer. His mother kept the car with her, as she needed it for her own driving purposes. All of that was understandable, but Rivera still wished she could ride around with the top down in the summer so that everyone could see her with hair flying in the wind and laughing with Solomon. She was embarrassed to be feeling that way, and she surely did not want Solomon to know her thoughts.

Amazingly, it turned into a summer to remember. She and Solomon bonded so well and found it so much fun just walking in the parks, hiking in the nearby woods, and sitting on a blanket having picnics. It was the deep conversations that intrigued Rivera. Dreaming about their future made so many possibilities seem to be right there in front of them. Solomon was a romantic. He told Rivera that he could see her driving a Mercedes Benz and stepping out of it with a black jaguar on a leash, while walking with tall pumps and a fitted jumpsuit with a drop-down halter top back. As all the men gathered around, he would walk up with his own cat on a leash and claim his lady. Rivera thought he had gone off the deep end, but she just laughed anyway as if she enjoyed his vision. Solomon said that he had already picked the college that he planned to attend and that he would be going to law school. Solomon had a way of speaking on such a high intellectual level, like he had researched many deep topics about law, politics, world views, and so many other things that it made her feel somewhat inadequate. Rivera thought he must have been exposed to many new things and brilliant intellectuals to be on the level he displayed. They agreed to stay in touch and commit themselves as boyfriend and girlfriend. It did not feel like a love match to Rivera, but she went along with it because she was intrigued by Solomon. There was no other boy in town who had challenged her intellect the way Solomon did, and it felt good and different.

Time seemed to speed by and they both were off to college in different states. The distance grew as they both had their own lives and careers. Rivera was very popular in college and was discovering her self-worth and character traits, which seemed a little different from what Solomon was wielding. Rivera called Solomon and suggested that they both concentrate on school and continue by planning their own separate lives. Solomon sounded hurt, but he came out with the most profound words. "Okay, baby love. I just want you to be happy, and if you are not happy, I cannot be happy." He also said, "There is no loss here, Rivera. One cannot lose something that they never had, and I must have never had you. It was only my illusion." Rivera was stunned, and she heard the phone disconnect. She always kept those words in her mind as she continued on with her life and career.

Rivera finished college and started her career. She thought about the vision that Solomon had with the Mercedes Benz and could not believe that it had come true. She thought, *Dreaming is seeing it, and believing will deliver it.* She purchased a new Mercedes 190E, a new model that was economically priced at the time. Of course, the vision about the black jaguar did not come true, as that was a figment of Solomon's deep imagination. It was Solomon's dream and not her dream to have a black jaguar. Rivera was terrified of cats, especially exotic and wild cats. She had heard over the years since they had spoken that Solomon finished law school and was a very successful lawyer. He had attended some type of military academy. He had been appointed as a judge. He seemed to be following his dream. Rivera had tried to contact him at a number that his mother provided, but he did not answer, so she never had any communication with him over the years.

"Grandma!"

"Oh, what is it, Rivenna?" Rivera had to snap back to the present as she heard Rivenna screaming at her. "Oh, sorry, Rivenna, I was just thinking back to when I was your age and about my life back then. These are the tender and impressionable years, Rivenna, and you must enjoy them while they last. This is the time when history is made during youth. It shapes the pathway for the future years. That is why I want to help design the best float for this great homecoming experience. These memories will last a lifetime. Why were you screaming at me like that, Rivenna?"

"I was trying to get your attention to let you know that the mailman was at the door. He had a certified letter for you, but I signed for it since it seemed like you were preoccupied in your thoughts. Here is the letter I signed for."

"Oh, thank you so much, Rivenna. I had really gone back into the time trails of my mind. Looking at you and the excitement of homecoming took me back to when I was your age."

Rivera looked at the letter coming from Solomon Craven, Esq. & Associates and wondered, *Oh no. What could this be?* It was an invitation to come to an event, the congressional announcement party for Solomon Craven. He was running for Congress. Oh my, this was some news for Rivera's ears. It was exciting as she thought about her memory of Solomon. So many different thoughts bombarded her mind at once. She wondered if she should make the trip to the party or just let the past be the past. Should she just let Solomon continue on his path of success? She should focus on getting this float done for the homecoming parade.

The float was so beautiful. It looked like a botanical garden floating in the clouds, with a big rainbow arched over the top. There were so many beautiful real and silk flowers. Rivera had picked the most redolent flowers, and the fragrance from the float lit up the air like a perfumed windstorm. Rivera designed the float to stimulate all five senses of sight, smell, touch, hearing, and taste. The sight of the float was breathtaking. The smell was fragrant like sweet perfume. There was a floral and refreshment display. One of the band members was standing next to the refreshment display playing melodic music on the violin. The flora and refreshment display were available for touch and purchase. There was an assortment of homemade tea cakes and banana, zucchini, and apple muffins available for purchase. There was also coffee and tea. The float was like a floating amusement attraction and also a fundraiser. It was so creative the way Rivera designed the presentation. The float won first place, and Rivenna was stunning, like a glowing ornament that adorned the top of a masterpiece. It was the best homecoming ever. Rivera felt happy and invigorated, as she was on to the next adventure.

Rivera decided to go to the announcement party. She was so nervous and could not stop trembling once the plane landed. She did not know what to expect. Had he changed? How different might Solomon look and act?

Solomon looked really good. He looked like he had been working out in the gym. He was mature and confident.

The party was well organized, and Solomon seemed to have much support. It was so different though. She thought it was something pulled deep from the trenches of Solomon's visionary landscape. There was a large platform on the stage with the words "Together we will do this. We will make it happen. If we can, we will. If each one can reach one. If each one can teach one." She sat and listened to the speech about a new Congress, a new way of doing things. She thought Solomon had gone off the deep end again. He talked about the House and sounded like he was trying to paint the picture of every house in the country becoming the House of Congress. He was trying to get each person to think about every family in a house coming together to agree on the main thing that was needed in their town or community. Then he told them to act like they were the congress to make it happen. He stated with strong affirmation and confirmation, "It is about more than just voting now! It is time for you to do what needs to be done for your community and stop pointing fingers at what the leaders are not doing." He described it like the times when someone might give you something. "The something may be what they want to give you, but the something is not really what you need. Does the something that they want you to have really help you? Should it really be called a gift of something if it is not what you really need to move forward? It leaves you stuck with accepting it and trying to adjust and be happy with it. Another example is when you donate something. Why would you give away something that has no value anymore? Why would you give someone your worst? Would you want someone to give you their worst? Now there is a time when a scrap builder may ask for your scraps. If that is the case, if scraps are what the person really needs, then that works. It is time to get what you need and want and not what someone else wants you to have. It is time that we get done what really needs to be gotten done, and nobody knows their needs better that you yourself. It is time to take a stand for your defined purpose in life. So, it is time to stop complaining and know that you can and will do this." He described it as e pluribus unum. "Out of one there will be many, out of many there will be one, one big congress made of many. We have the power to do this. Together we will make this happen. Together we will get this done."

Everybody was on their feet clapping and cheering. Rivera stood clapping also because she was so proud of Solomon, and his message was stimulating. However, she thought it all sounded good, but she wondered how Solomon was planning on getting something this different accomplished. It was a totally different model than what already existed. He had so many new ideas and concepts, and he had step-by-step models to follow and adapt to, depending on what the exact needs of the community were. He also seemed to have the power and influence to give the green light to go forward once all the houses came together in agreement on the most important issues. That model seemed to have many detailed plans of action to follow. Each house is a congress. Then he showed the models of how to move to the next most important issue step by step. Each time a house achieved the goal of solving an issue, the announcement would be broadcasted like a top news story, and other communities and their houses would know about the accomplishments. Solomon predicted that it would be different, as it might feel like you were in another land like the promised land, as life had not seen progress of this magnitude. The crowd could not stop cheering.

As the party was ending, Rivera went to try to speak to Solomon, but he had so many people around him she could not get near. As she was finally making her way out of the building and back to the hotel, she heard footsteps and felt a tap on her shoulder. She turned around, and to her surprise, it was Solomon. They hugged like they were lifelong lost friends. Rivera congratulated him on the speech, platform, and quest for the new congress. He told her that the reason he had sent the letter to invite her was he wanted her to join his campaign team. He felt that she knew best how he thought and could connect to his visions with the energy necessary to move this vision forward. He said, "Rivera, you were my river that gave me my flow. I have always loved and sincerely appreciated what you gave me during the time I needed someone the most. You sat by me and handled those bullies on the bus that night."

She felt honored that he had considered her in that way after all these years. He told her that the bond that they made together as teenagers had been the inspiration for his life and all pursuits, even though their lives had gone separate ways. He said it was not until he got older and wiser that he truly realized the power of dreaming and envisioning the future during the young years to prepare for the years to come. Conceiving it and believing it is what makes it happen. "Thank you, Rivera, for being a part of my dreams back then. Please consider continuing it now." Solomon also said that he had been meeting with a dynamic husband and wife team that would be helping him, Mr. and Mrs. Carter Fulston. He said, "Rivera, I really feel in my heart that you are the missing piece to this, and I need you by my side. You will meet the rest of the team if you come to the next planning meeting."

Rivera was brought to tears and said yes, she would be honored to be a part of something like that at that time in her life. He gave her his business card and asked her to contact his office for the next planning meeting. Rivera went back to the hotel room to chart out the next stage of her life. She was still in awe at the thought of something this magnificent and magnanimous. She had to make some moves soon to accommodate this new project, which was different from the career path she had chosen many years ago. She just kept thinking to herself, *If I can, I will do it. Together it can happen.*

Breakdown of Key Components from the Story

Now this is a story of true *visionary determination, will, perseverance,* evolving, *passion,* courage, and so many more of the scripts. The bonds made early in life are like seeds planted for the future that connect to what is destined to happen. The story can be a mystery because even though the vision may be foreseen, there can also be so many unpredictable elements. Just think of the greatness, potential, and impact that was stored inside that scared little boy back on the bus who could not stand up to the bullies that wanted to take his seat. Now he was striving to create a new kind of seat that those bullies would not want to have any part of. Solomon put out the challenge for everyone to go deep and pull from and use all of the scripts available to them. The way Solomon's vision came together is with the belief that one person may not be able to do everything, but each one can do something. That something combined with the somethings from each and every other person builds the gigantic congress that becomes everything that each person needs to keep doing something. It may seem complex, but it is a brilliant way to tap into all the scripts defined to each individual person and use them to keep harvesting and harnessing more scripts. *A bond made early in life could seal the deal for life and could be unstoppable.*

A Piece of Peace

Dessa Winhands screamed in dismay when she got the letter from the mailbox. Her worst fear had just been delivered. It was the year 1966. Dessa had feared getting the letter right after she attended Rogers High School graduation. Graduation was supposed to be a happy and proud occasion, but Dessa just could not stop thinking about what the future would hold for Rogers. The Vietnam War was alive, and there was a mandatory draft in place. So many young boys never made it back home. Dessa felt in her gut that Rogers would be chosen soon for the draft. The confirmation of that fear just came like a big punch to the gut. Dessa stood holding the letter and wondered how she should break the news to Rogers. He would be devastated because Dessa believed that Rogers was planning on asking for Clementine's hand in marriage. He was such a quiet gentleman and wanted to honor Clementine with marriage before trying to start a family.

Rogers Winhands was a peacemaker and always tried to do the right thing. He never raised his voice or seemed to get upset. If he was worried about something, he kept it to himself until it worked its way out. Dessa remembered when Rogers was eating watermelon. Somehow, Rogers had gotten a seed stuck in his ear. Rogers was around eight years old then. She noticed that he just quietly walked around with his head turned to the side like he was trying to pour a drink of water from his ear. He never said a word about what was wrong. One day, his oldest sister, Sherenta, got a glimpse of something inside Rogers's ear. Sherenta got a hair pin and started trying to extract whatever it was. Sherenta kept digging and finally got it out. It was a watermelon seed.

That was why Dessa dreaded delivering the painful news to Rogers. Clementine would be upset. She seemed to really love Rogers. Anyone who knew Rogers loved him because he was a very fine man who would make such a great husband and father. He would be a great catch for any young woman. He was responsible and diligent. He also was very kind. Mr. Bakers at the Seed House where Rogers worked could not stop singing praises about him. Mr. Bakers said that Rogers was his best worker. He said that Rogers just quietly paced himself, and what seemed like a big mountain got reduced to a small mole hill because of the way Rogers did the work. "His ethics are just outstanding," Mr. Baker said.

Dessa finally broke the news to her son. It brought her to tears to see the expression on Rogers's face as he read the draft notice that came in the mail. Rogers did not react as if he was unhappy or upset, because that was the peaceful way he was. He did not want to upset his mother any more than she already was. He was kind of afraid to tell Clementine because he knew that she really wanted to get married. He just hoped she would have faith and wait until he had served his term and returned home.

Well the day came to send Rogers away to service, there was not a dry eye anywhere. Clementine could not stop crying. Dessa tried to hide her tears, but they kept flowing. Sherenta was sniffling. The Continental Trailways bus looked like a giant hearse with many seats headed to slaughter. It was hard to see it in any other way, knowing that Rogers was going to war and was getting on that bus. Rogers stood strong though and just waved goodbye. Clementine stood there in shock. Dessa felt like her heart had dropped to her stomach. Clementine was dropped off back at her house after they left the bus station. She jumped out of the car and ran to her door like she was running for her life.

Clementine ran away so fast because she did not believe that Rogers would come back to her. She must have been crying desperately and painfully because she let out a loud wailing scream just before she got to the door to her house. She fell to the ground and had to crawl inside.

So many young men's lives had been taken away, and the promise of love and a family had been obliterated by the sound of a cannon signaling war. It hurt Dessa to think about Rogers being out there in a strange country and enemy territory when he was so mild mannered and peaceful. If he could not pick a watermelon seed from his ear, how would he fight someone or be a quick draw with a gun?

Dessa cried and prayed every night, just trying to find a piece of peace. She asked as humbly and as sincerely as she could, while on her knees each night, "Lord, please take care of Rogers. Dear God, please stop the war and bring our boys home alive."

A year later, Dessa received another notice in the mail. It was not a letter about the draft; it was an invitation to a wedding. Dessa could not believe her eyes. Clementine was marrying Butler Garfield. Butler had worked with Rogers down at the Seed House. He must have made his move on Clementine soon after Rogers left. He must have taken advantage of her being sad and lonely. There was also a baby shower invitation in the envelope. Dessa held her anger because she wanted to stay focused and peaceful in her request to God to bring Rogers back home alive and in one piece, with all body parts attached. She wished the best for Clementine. She knew that Rogers would find someone else who truly loved him and would wait for him even if he went to the moon.

Six months later, Dessa went to the mailbox and received another letter. Her heart was in her throat when she saw the envelope. Her hands trembled so that she could hardly open the envelope. Dessa dropped the envelope in a mud puddle on the way back to the house from the mailbox. She decided she better wait to get inside and sit down first. Dessa could not open the letter until she reached out to God first with a prayer. Dessa prayed that whatever news was in the letter, just please give her the strength to handle it. Dessa finally opened the letter to read it. It was a little hard reading through the mud stains on the paper. She saw clearly what it was saying though. Rogers had received a minor gun powder wound, and he was back in the States now and not in Vietnam. He had completed eleven months and twenty-one days on the battlefield, and he was being granted an honorable discharge. Dessa howled, screamed, and jumped with joy and gratitude, thankful for the gift that had just been delivered to her. She thanked God for granting her wish and for the delivery in the mail. She hollered for Sherenta, who came in running and jumping. Then Dessa thought about the dilemma that mighty make the celebration bittersweet, breaking the news to Rogers that Clementine had moved on and married someone else.

The day finally arrived when Rogers returned home. Dessa felt like she had been welcomed into heaven but was still on this earth and in her physical body. Yet it felt like she was out of her body and in a dreamlike state just looking at the sight of her handsome and honorable son. Rogers looked well.

The local church had planned a welcome-home reception. The small church was full and with standing room only to welcome Rogers back. He was asked to speak about how it felt to be back home. Rogers started giving the account of the incident that allowed him to return home.

He talked about the night he found the perfect spot to dig a foxhole to sleep for the night. He said it looked like a nice piece of land, similar to the field behind the Seed House, but the grass looked totally different there in the Vietnam jungle. Rogers said that he had dug his spot and was ready to get in to watch for any sign of the enemy. Then another soldier walked up and yelled at him, saying that the spot belonged to him. He said that he had picked out that spot first. Rogers looked at the soldier in disbelief and did not argue. Rogers felt in his heart that the soldier wanted the spot because it was already dug and ready to go. It was ready for the soldier to just get in, and he would not have to put in any work or do any digging. Rogers remembered his work ethic at the Seed House, and he just peacefully said to the soldier, "Go ahead, man, and take this spot. I will find another spot."

Rogers went as far away from that spot as he could and dug another foxhole for himself. He said a prayer and tried to relax as best as possible under the hostile circumstances. It was enough to watch for and fight the enemy; he surely did not want to have friendly fire with a member of his own platoon. Rogers made it through the night. The next morning, the soldier who took the first spot that Rogers had dug was found blown to pieces. A bomb had detonated underneath that hole. Rogers gasped a choking breath once he heard the news. He thought to himself, *That was like a piece of peace.* Even in the face of war, peace was found by his peacefully agreeing to let the other soldier have that piece of land for his foxhole. Hopefully, but sadly, that soldier was resting in peace in the unknown, and Rogers was peacefully standing there speaking to a church full of supporters at home. Rogers felt so blessed, yet he always wondered if that was what life had destined for the other soldier. It saddened him to think about what and how it happened. The whole audience was on their feet, jumping and shouting and giving thanks for the gift that had been delivered and for the light of omnipotent love that story and experience brightly reflected to the world. Just hearing that story gave hope to all the supporters that God was going to deliver another gift and the war would be over soon.

Breakdown of Key Components from the Story

Now this is another story to be told and remembered. It has so many components to it, and it pulled from the scripts of *faith, hope, love,* and *peace.* There is so much goodness pulled from the sounding board also. It is about *will* and *determination.* It is about *dedication* and service. Again, a gift was granted on demand and delivered. The birth of Rogers Winhands delivered by Dessa Winhands had stored within Rogers the DNA code and characteristic of peace. A peaceful child was born, and that script was used and needed in the face of war. The mandatory draft seemed like a very dark script, but it was meant for Rogers to bring peace in the face of war. That is like pure Greatness On Demand—Granted On Delivery (GOD on the sound platform). The scripts unfolded and showed up right on time. The greatest gift had been opened. *A piece of peace begins with peace.*

The Trail through the Veil— Step Back, Holler Back

Darlene Mason felt like a zombie walking around with broken bones and dripping wounds all over her body. It felt so empty and hollow inside, as a part of her had recently departed. Darlene looked around the room as she packed the belongings in preparation for the estate sale for Luttie Rae. She could not believe that Luttie Rae was gone. The house had so many memories and was once bubbling with fun, laughter, kindness, hope, and delicious family meals. It was hard to conceive that Luttie Rae was in another place. Darlene wished she knew if Luttie Rae was okay. It just did not seem real that she was gone. Luttie Rae was such a peaceful and beautiful person with a spirit of gold. She should have lasted more than a hundred years on this earth. She had so much to give, and she gave her entire life to help so many people. Luttie Rae was the best sister that Darlene could have ever imagined. The love between the siblings was so strong. Darlene had organized the final table of household goods when she spotted Luttie Rae's favorite purse with all her belongings left inside, just as they were on the day she departed. Darlene decided to keep the purse as a keepsake and not include it in the estate sale. She could see so clearly in her mind Luttie Rae getting the purse to walk out the door for work or to go to the supermarket. The scene in her mind felt like a valuable commodity and a memory that would last forever.

Darlene paused and took a deep breath to try to regroup. Darlene wished she understood the entire process of life, creation, and purpose. She wondered when the season of sadness would stop reigning and raining so much pain. Her heart felt like it was shattered into so many pieces after the loss of Luttie Rae, and now Darlene had another mountain to climb. She needed to get to the nursing home to say her final goodbye to her lifetime friend, Veronica Blessing. The pain felt unbearable, and the sadness was earth-shattering. Luttie Rae and now Veronica.

Darlene thought about the memories that she and Veronica shared. Darlene remembered the day she decided to introduce Veronica to her friend and coworker Carlton Blessing. Veronica and Carlton seemed to hit it off right away. They dated for more than a year and appeared to be inseparable. Finally, Carlton said that he did not want to live without Veronica and asked for her hand in marriage. They got married, and a year later, a beautiful baby girl was born. Veronica had thought that she could not have children because she had not conceived and she was almost forty years old. The love between her and Carlton proved that to be a myth. It happened right before her fortieth birthday. The baby girl was so beautiful. She looked like a little doll. Darlene was reflecting on the memory of the scene as Veronica smiled with so much joy and love for her daughter and Carlton. Then Carlton burst into tears as he held his little baby girl. Darlene thought about how blessed it was that Carlton and Veronica found each other and lived so happily for more than twenty years.

Carlton had passed away three years ago, and Veronica had taken the loss with the strength that stood from their love, yet with much sadness. Now Veronica was getting ready to take her last stand. Darlene had visited Veronica the week before, as many friends and family had come to say their final goodbyes. Darlene had held Veronica's hand and looked at her wounded body. It was hard to believe that a disease could cause the loss of limbs in that way. There was nothing else to be done but continue cutting, and Veronica felt that it was enough. She declared that she did not want to undergo any more surgeries. Darlene remembered Veronica's riveting words of declaration, "I have won this race, and Thy will be done!" Veronica was always a very strong person whose company friends and family loved. She was kind, yet she did not mind speaking her mind. She was the best wife for Carlton, as they complemented each other. Veronica and Darlene had done so many things together as lifetime friends. Veronica was there to help when Darlene's mother passed away. Veronica styled the wig for Darlene's mother to wear during the final viewing. Veronica was always doing good things for so many people. She had an instinctive way of knowing just what to do at the right time to help others. Darlene felt so blessed to have lived and known her sister, Luttie Rae, and her friend Veronica. How uncanny it felt to be losing two of the greatest people in the world so soon behind each other. It did not feel real.

As Darlene walked into the room at the nursing facility to say the final goodbye to Veronica, she felt so weak, as if she was about to pass out. She thought of what Veronica and Luttie Rae must have been feeling as they knew the end was about to appear. Darlene mustered up enough strength to walk to Veronica's bed. Veronica appeared to be sleeping, as she was breathing through the oxygen mask and the machine that had been provided by the hospice team. Veronica turned her head to see who was coming in the room, and Darlene knew that Veronica felt her presence. Veronica's awareness of her loved ones was always so keen, no matter what she was going through herself. Darlene grabbed Veronica's hand. Darlene said, "Veronica, I love you. Thank you for a wonderful lifetime of friendship."

Darlene could feel Veronica squeezing her hand as she spoke the best words to Veronica that her mind could muster with the painful circumstance at hand. It felt so painful for Darlene to see Veronica in that weakened state, as Veronica had been so full of life all her life. It was just so hard to say goodbye. Darlene then said, "Veronica, please find Luttie Rae and ask her if she can find a way to let me know if she is doing okay with her continued journey of life." Veronica usually relished the thought of doing what someone asked her to do, especially if she felt that it served a good purpose. "Please tell Luttie Rae that I love her so much. Veronica, I am trying to be strong, as you have been such an inspiration of strength for me, and I will cherish that forever."

Veronica appeared to not hear Darlene and just solemnly continued trying to breathe through that oxygen mask. She appeared to be making her way to the pathway to the other world. Darlene started to walk out of the room because she was trembling with tears. The pain was just too hard to bear as the memories of life flooded Darlene's mind, body, and soul. Darlene had walked out into the hallway when she heard her name being called. She looked around to see who in the hallway was speaking to her. There was no one in the hallway. Darlene turned around and looked back to Veronica's room and realized it may have been Veronica who called her name. Darlene walked to Veronica's bed and could not believe the sound that was radiating to her ears. It was the sound of Veronica's voice delivering a message. Veronica said, "Luttie Rae say she is doing okay, but she will be coming back because she left her purse. She needs to get her purse." Darlene then heard Veronica greet someone else, and her last words were, "Hey, Mama, give me a hug." The scene in the room weakened yet strengthened Darlene at the same time. She could not believe what had just happened. It was like Veronica was traveling down the pathway through the trail to the other existence. She kept one foot back in the realm where Darlene was so that she could holler back and deliver the message from Luttie Rae. Then Veronica just disappeared through the veil on the trail to meet her mother and other loved ones and friends. Darlene felt sad but realized a very powerful gift had been delivered to her that she would cherish for a lifetime.

"What just happened?" The powerful gift that remained was the ability of Veronica to step back across to the physical world and holler a message from beyond. That was so powerful and almost unbelievable, but it happened.

Breakdown of Key Components from the Story

This was such a touching story that pulled from many different dimensions and scripts. It had *power* in a time of sorrow. The lifetime of memories and *goodwill* seemed to be a part of what would continue to the next stage of life for Luttie Rae and Veronica. It also appeared that a message back to earth was that each would continue working and live again by coming back or working from the other dimension. There seemed to be a very thin line between the veils of existence. This story is chilling yet gives a type of *hope* to ponder. *The miracle of birth and life is riddled with the discovery of miracles all around.*

Teardrops from the Light

It had been a long and tiring day. I had gotten up early to prepare for a trip with my sister, Doris; her husband, James; and their daughter, Naiomi. I felt nervous and anxious as I thought about visiting with my beautiful sisters at the graveside. My oldest sister, Versia, passed away in November 2015, and my next oldest sister, Lucy, passed away in November 2018. Their lives seemed very short to me. Lucy was only sixty-nine years old, and Versia was only seventy-two years old. I wished they could have lived forever in the physical realm, even though they will live forever in my heart and mind. They were buried side by side at the same cemetery. They were the two oldest sisters and were the trailblazers for the rest of the family. They gave so much love, wisdom, and emotional support. They were the older sisters, and it did not take long for them to step into their roles within our family structure. They assumed parenting roles for the younger siblings. This was necessary because our parents were older and born during a time where there was not much opportunity to thrive economically. There were eight children born. Our family came together in support of one another to survive with pure love and togetherness. All we had was one another. Their lives, memories, contributions, and pure love sometimes seem like a guiding light tucked away in my heart but shining each day as I try to move forward with my own life. The loss of beautiful souls like my sisters is painful and takes time to process. It is a daily journey.

The anticipation of going to the graveside felt weird in a way. It was excruciating to put a meaning to the emotional uproar that was stirring inside me. It was not the first time I had visited the site. My sister Doris and I had been dedicated to visiting the grave site and supporting the perpetual care for the sacred resting place of our sisters. We had visited many times since the burials, yet each time seemed like a new journey. The state of grief felt familiar yet different each time. The anticipation drew anxiousness each time a visit was planned.

I am so grateful for their lives and so blessed with the gift of being their sister. Both of my sisters that have transitioned were unique. They both mastered the sounding board that I have described in this book. Many days, their obstacles seemed unsurmountable, but they both lived to conquer many and to have the best quality of life possible. I sat there just thinking about all the stories of daily life and how the scripts were wielded to get through the tasks on their journeys. I felt sad but tried to tell myself that the transition they had made was peaceful. I still felt the need to find something that would make the strange emotion that I was feeling inside of me settle down. I had the idea that I would talk to them at the graveside as if they were listening, just as I talked with them when they lived. I thought of the burial site as a branch of knowledge in the earth. Many times, I sit in thought and reflect about the many beautiful lives that have transitioned and wish that their wisdom could be called upon at will, like a flowing, natural resource. It is my opinion that all the wisdom buried in the earth is like the closing of a large library or university that inspired millions of learners and seekers during their lifetime. That is the inspiration I feel when I think of all the knowledge, kindness, and love that they gave to me. It seemed like getting an additional degree of education in a field that has not been defined yet in school. It is so humbling and inspiring to think of the lifetime transformations that can manifest by this type of edification. The love is so pure that it feels like it embellishes your soul and is the backbone of your existence. It inspires hope. Their care, concern, hugs, and smiles brought peace to me and many others. Being in their presence captured the beauty of life in a single snapshot.

The time finally arrived to walk the pathway to the burial site, the branch of knowledge in the earth. We stood together around the grave and prayed. The prayer lit a spark inside of Naiomi, my sister's seven-year-old daughter. She started praying and thanking Lucy for being the best person ever. She said, "You are the very best, and your sisters standing here are the best. You are the best ever, and I love you so much. I hate you had to die, but you will always live inside me and be remembered as the best to ever live." Hearing those words coming from the mouth of that little one made my legs tremble and eyes water. The words were so sincere and pure. I then began to speak to Lucy and Versia. I asked them to rise and help the family get through this. I asked them in a very sincere and heart-throbbing plea to please let me know if they could hear me. I asked them to please send me a sign to let me know if there is any knowledge and power buried in the grave that I might be connecting to. The visit felt enlightening, and as if a small burden had been lifted off. I was glad to get the visit over with and was ready to get to the hotel to relax.

I felt famished and drained. It is a normal pattern for me to fast when a visit of that nature is planned. For me, the fasting makes the portal inside feel more open to transmit and receive. It has been a practice that I have done since the age of eleven. I discovered it when my cousin had an injury that caused pneumonia to set in. It turned into a critical situation for my beautiful cousin. The family was called in to say the final goodbyes. The shocking and unexpected news had the young Debra so scared and worried. I remember being so frightened that I did not have an appetite. It pained my heart to hear the crying from my cousin's mother and the words, "I know God would not do this. Please let her live." We were all so close and powered by pure love. I felt that there must be something I could do. I asked my mother and my cousin's mother if I could visit with my cousin alone. I remember the anticipation and some fear rumbling inside when I saw the intensive care room. I was alone, but it felt like I had something inside of me to deliver. I prayed, talked to, and held my cousin's hand.

My cousin was conscious, and she said, "Thank you, Deb. You got a strong spirit." Those words made me cry. I had no idea that a turning point was afoot. The light turned on, and a gift was delivered. My cousin survived the day and the night and did not die. The imminent death prediction was upgraded to stable condition, and the next week, my cousin came home. It was a miracle!

Now back to the current moment. The feelings felt familiar, like those more than forty years ago when my cousin was so ill, a miracle was delivered, and she recovered.

We left the cemetery and went to the hotel. I still did not have an appetite to eat. I just wanted to relax. I checked into my room, got comfortable in bed, and fell asleep. I had no idea what time it was and how long I had been sleeping when I heard the shower running. I immediately turned over and thought, *Someone is taking a shower.* The thought finally resonated clearly in my mind. *Debra, you are the only one in the room. If you are in the bed sleeping, who is taking a shower?* I felt a little nervous as I thought about it. I needed to get up and see who was in the shower. I picked up my cell phone to call for help, but I dropped it by the time I made it to the bathroom door. My cell phone's camera was on video to try to record, but it only got a few seconds of the sound of the water dripping in the shower. I looked inside the bathroom at the shower and tub, and to my surprise, no person was visible in the shower. This was a big OMG moment—"Oh my God!" The water was pouring from the bulb-encased light that was mounted in the ceiling over the bathtub. It was streaming down like a flowing spring. The water was dropping from the outer circular rim of the light like teardrops or raindrops. It was not raining outside, and even if it was, the room was not on the top floor of the hotel. As the drops started to fall not as fluently, a thought nudged me to get the camera phone and film it. A video record of this was necessary to prove that this was happening for real. I thought that if I told someone about this and did not have a picture or video, people would think that I was dreaming or making up a story.

I filmed the light showering or dropping teardrops and felt a little anxious but not really frightened. I took pictures of the light and the bathtub area. I got back in bed once it stopped and thought about calling the front desk to see if a maintenance person was on duty. I wanted to get an explanation for what happened. When the maintenance person arrived, the water had stopped dripping from the light. I showed the video and pictures to the maintenance person. He said that he would check downstairs to see if the tub had overflowed in the room below. I was so confused by that statement, so I asked, "How can a tub on the floor below overflow up to the ceiling in my room?"

He then replied, "Oh, I mean I will go and check the floor above to see if there is a problem." I waited to get a phone call or for them to come back and tell me what happened, but no one called to give me a report of the findings.

When morning finally arrived, I decided to call the front desk and ask about the maintenance report. I was informed that the trouble report had been closed. I asked the attendant, "What was the problem?" because no one had come back to the room to fix the light leak. I was informed that there was not a problem. The attendant said that no problem was found on either floor. My heart then started to beat very fast. I asked the attendant if she could please get a copy of the report. The attendant said that it was against policy to give the customer the report. I asked the attendant if management approval could be gotten for me. I wanted to have a written statement that confirmed that the problem was checked out and no leak on either floor was found. I went down to the front desk and was given a simple statement written on the hotel letterhead. I communicated to the hotel staff that I was not trying to be difficult. It was that if there was no real-life answer, then I felt in my heart that the occurrence was from the supernatural realm. It meant that I had just witnessed a current and live phenomenon. I felt a warm feeling inside and wondered if that was the sign being sent from beyond, delivered from the branch of knowledge. The shower was heard about nine hours after the visit to the branch of knowledge.

From the looks on the faces of the staff, they were spooked. The word had traveled fast about the incident. Questions were being asked, so I pulled out my cell phone and showed the video. Many reactions started to be spoken out loud, and it seemed that emotions were being stimulated. One person said, "I am not scared because I know God." Another said something strange had happened to them before and started telling the story of their experience. I saw someone else take off running toward the back, as if they did not want to hear the rest of the conversation. It had turned into something like a scary Halloween outing. That was not the intention that I had when I reported the incident. I initially thought that the water might be coming from a malfunction or a leak somewhere.

I decided to go back to her room and let my sister and her husband know about what had occurred during the night. The maid came to my door and knocked. She wanted to see if I would be checking out. I thought that was strange because it was not even nine in the morning, and checkout was not until 11:00 a.m. It was just a little after six thirty. My sister Doris heard me talking outside in the hallway and came to my room to see what I was talking about. I showed both my sister Doris and the maid the video. Then I noticed something else on the scene that was unexplainable. The stopper was secured tightly in the bathtub, and the water that had dropped from the light was not there in the bathtub. The bathtub was bone-dry. Doris asked the maid if she could please bend down and inspect the tub to witness that the tub was dry. The maid bent down and touched the tub with shaky hands and legs.

Doris then realized that the scene was scaring the maid. The maid admitted that Debra's account of what happened was scaring her. Then Doris turned around and screamed in shock. The cart that the maid used for cleaning the rooms had an insulated lunch bag hanging on it that looked just like Lucy's lunch bag. Lucy was the sister who had recently passed away. Doris remembered that she had been using the lunch bag for several months after Lucy passed. It had recently torn apart from carrying heavy bottles of water in it. Doris had discontinued using the bag and discarded it. The bag on the cleaning cart was a replica of the bag that Lucy owned. Also, another observation was that the name engraved on the cleaning cart, which was the same name that the maid had on her name tag, was coincidentally the name of one of Lucy's high school classmates. I took a picture of the strange coincidence, the bag that looked just like Lucy's bag. It appeared to me that the bag was an additional confirmation of the supernatural communication speaking to me in a visual way in the field of the current surroundings.

I left the bathroom tub and shower area just as it was. Inside my mind and heart, I silently labeled it a sacred place where history had just been made. I thought about asking the hotel management to not rent the sacred room to anyone in the future, but I decided it may turn into something too complicated to pursue.

I felt renewed and buzzing with energy and awe after what had happened. I could not wait to share the story. Some of the people who have been lifelong friends of the family had some very good insights. Others seemed to be in disbelief. One very good family friend, Pastor Jerrel Coleman, suggested I read Exodus 17:1–7. The passage refers to Moses going to the rock at Horeb and striking the rock to make water because the people who were in the Desert of Sin were thirsty for water. The people were quarreling with Moses and demanded that he give them water to drink.

Jerrel Coleman interpreted this passage and offered it as a reading to console and affirm what had happened. She said if God can make water come out of the rocks, she believed it was the hand of God that dropped the water from the light. She prayed with the family and believed that the message was that the water was the purification process from the pain and grief. The light continuing to shine and not burn out even though water was dripping from it was saying to not be sad or worry; just follow the light of God, and the light will always shine the pathway. She also said that it was a way to let the family know that Lucy and Versia were fine, and they did not want the family to be sad and worry.

There were many nice and supportive things said by many who heard the story.

Each day, thoughts come to me about the scene at the hotel. The way the water dripped from the light and dried before it hit the tub was like drying tears before they fell from the eyes. Then the fact that the light over the tub was still shining brightly after all the teardrops had fallen was astonishing. It really did seem like a sign of the purification process of the pain to wipe all the tears away and let the light shine. It was uplifting to my spirit. It felt like a burden had been lifted. I sincerely felt that the branch of wisdom had spoken in an omnipotent and loving way. That is the power of omnipotent love!

Breakdown of Key Components from the Story

Now this story gives meaning to the whole process of the blueprint from the creation delivered at birth, through the life cycle on the journey, to the glimmers of light that direct the path of life and beyond. The reflections from the many beams of light on the journey are testimonials of the mighty, the omnipotence, the *love* that has powered generation after generation after generation with the shining light. The scripts are all inside and have the power to radiate all around. It is no wonder that a reflection may reflect backward into the space on the trail that it once navigated and explored. It is sometimes referred to as history repeating itself. The trail bearing tears, heartaches, and heartbreaks, sweetened with subtle joys, is blazed with memories powered by the rays shining from the beacon of light. The flame of the torch has been passed to the ones left behind. It is a story of *power, love, courage,* and *compassion.*

The Showering Light

Let It Shine

The pain of the loss tugged and filled my heart.
Letting go of you so soon was very hard to part.
Trying to face the situation did not seem real.
The reality and finality I didn't want to feel.
The remains of your life are buried deep in the earth,
The body of your shell storing the seeds from birth.
If there is any knowledge, hear me now and rise;
The sign was delivered right before my eyes.
I have always heard "ask and you shall receive."
You reaffirmed that truth to see and believe.
The granted wish flowing through the shower,
What a real testament to the supernatural power.
Teardrops dropping steadily from the light,
The serenading sound stimulating the sight.
Oh, what a sight as teardrops fade away,
But the shining light beaming here to stay.
Drip, drop, drip, drop—hearing the sounds tonight,
Bringing goodness and love and shining so bright.
Thank you for your presence; now I feel all right.
Ole hooray to the showering light
From beyond the unknown that leaves one to ponder.

The message is sent, so there is no need to wonder.
Granted on delivery, open the greatest gift.
Let your bright light shine in spirit and uplift.

This poem was composed on October 25, 2019, in memory of and with gratitude for the supernatural phenomenon witnessed on October 13, 2019.

Opening the Greatest Gift

The delivery into the world from the mother's womb brings a new creation to life. Each creation has its own set of blueprints. Even identical twins that shared the same sac in the womb and come out looking almost exactly alike have their own set of unique characteristics that make their blueprints different. The birth of a new creation is a miracle, and many miracles unfold during life. These miracles are stored within each creation, and the journey during life holds the key to opening the miracle. The miracle was granted to each creation during delivery, but it is left up to each creation to open the greatest gift tucked and stored deeply in the vaults of each existence. How can one get to the vault?

The Light

At birth, the creation is born and delivered into the world. The outside body and the inside network of all the cells and organs that power the outside body and overall health grow from a baby to an adult. The characteristics and traits of the person and the physical body shine into the world with the voice of the personality. The personality is what powers the beam of light to shine upon others. It is as if, along with the overall body, deep inside the DNA code, there was also a light delivered. The light can turn on the power to fight and heal when the invaders attack the body. It can show up as a gift to make things happen even when it appears that all is lost. It can be the gift that shines the light to help someone else see the path more clearly on their personal journey. When the light is used to shine upon someone else, the light makes another light that glows with the impact of the connection. It can be a heartwarming light. It can be a light of inspiration. It can be like a lightbulb that sparks ideas for others. It can be a light that powers energy to make things happen inside the person, or it can be the energy that brings the power for others to make things happen. In essence, even when the physical body has been reduced to the last remains, the light from the creation still shines. There have been many caretakers who witnessed the death of patients and reported seeing a light or glow in the room when the life exited the body. Left behind could be many light beams that spread from one single beam. This process may be repeated over and over again. The light was born with each creation. As that creation utilizes their gift of the light, it can spread more light to others who are also capable of shining their own lights. Beams of the light come together to form huge energy fields that can bring much power for unlimited possibilities to occur. These light beams shine through the generations of family and friends still living in the physical life. The cycle goes on and on. From one cell, many cells divide and make many more cells. From a tiny beam of light, many beams come together to make a strong and steadfast platform that shines the beacon of light. The guiding light shines and revolves as the world evolves. The greatest gift remains for each person to use the light inside and shine it to light the pathway, which may also light a path for others. The entire process of life is a gift to be used to discover the greatest gift.

The discovery is always waiting to be discovered. It can feel like falling in love when the discovery has been made. It can feel like an addiction to a special cause when the discovery has been made. It can feel like freedom when the discovery has been made. It can feel like peace when the discovery has been made. It can feel like being in excellent health when the discovery has been made. It can be the most beautiful sight ever seen. It can sound like the most melodious tune ever heard. The definition of the feeling, sight, or sound can be in your own words once it has been discovered. It can feel like a miracle. It can feel like the greatest gift has been opened. That gift was granted on the delivery of each new creation into the world. The delivery is what set up the greatest gift to be received. The little light was tucked inside of the delivery.

As all the different dimensions from past history of generations to the present life of new creations and all the components of the human construct; to the landscapes of the frontiers of the physical world; to the day-to-day real-life struggles and accomplishments on the journey— there is a supernatural element that may reveal itself as the guiding light that shines through the pathway of the exploration. When this happens, it is like a phenomenon, an anomaly that cannot be explained in the sense of the real world. Yet the phenomena entered the space and life of the real world. When something of this nature reveals itself, it can leave the mind in a ponderous state of confusion.

The sound platform has many scripts that each person has the freedom to call up and use at will. Each person is unique; therefore, their descriptions will be unique to who they are. That is what makes the world so great and diverse. If each person uses their scripts, they become the gifts of greatness that can cause the delivery of more gifts to be granted and delivered. Making the vow to commit to practicing using the scripts every day in whatever line of work, school, duty, business, or self-worth opens the portal to shine light through the darkest moments. The supply is granted on demand and delivered. Those are the keys to navigating life's adventures. Once this is mastered, if each one will reach one and if each one will teach one, the field of energy of light beams will be so bright. Many gifts can miraculously be opened. It may seem difficult at first, but just look around. If anyone has made it from the birth delivery as a baby to any year above twenty, a score, then just think how many gifts were delivered and opened to get that far. What is the greatest to be opened though? That greatest gift is like the biggest secret, the mystery of life. It is like going on a treasure hunt, and the hunt is your lifetime. The greatest gift was granted on the delivery of your birth, tucked inside the vehicle of life that carries you. The glimmer of the light sits, waiting to shine brightly.

The old phrase *seeing is believing and believing is seeing* holds scripts. To believe in your gift and to see it unfold and open makes one see and believe even more in the potential and possibilities of the self. The self is like its own self-entailed platform that can connect to many other platforms. One becomes many. Many become one. Once the gift has been granted on delivery and opened, it shines the greatest sense of purpose, and the perfect clarity.

About the Author

Debra Domino loves to write books that capture the everyday essence of real-life issues. Debra has been described as a creative and artistic author who writes passionately from the heart. She has a style that captures real life, and it is easy to feel the emotion of her stories. Through her own personal stories, she has seen many experiences that delivered messages. She has found that going to the quiet sometimes allows the messages to become visible and audible. Once a message has been received that gives vision, the gift of the awakening is priceless if it helps to move forward a necessary cause in a positive way. *Open Your Greatest Gift* is a continuation of the journey that started with the last composition, *Reflections of Omnipotent Love*. The author believes that the reflection of love is what allows the gifts to show up to be opened. Debra Domino is a contributing author in *Ready Aim Captivate*, *Wounded Survive Thrive*, and *My Creative Thoughts*.

Printed in the United States
By Bookmasters